Anonymus

Correspondence on Removal or Lighting of Daunt's Rock

Improvement of Roche's Light, Fog Signals and Approaches to Cork Harbour

1865-73

Anonymus

Correspondence on Removal or Lighting of Daunt's Rock
*Improvement of Roche's Light, Fog Signals and Approaches to Cork Harbour
1865-73*

ISBN/EAN: 9783742825940

Manufactured in Europe, USA, Canada, Australia, Japa

Cover: Foto ©Thomas Meinert / pixelio.de

Manufactured and distributed by brebook publishing software
(www.brebook.com)

Anonymus

Correspondence on Removal or Lighting of Daunt's Rock

DAUNT'S ROCK (CORK HARBOUR).

RETURN to an Order of the Honourable the House of Commons,
dated 24 March 1874 ;—for,

" COPIES of all Correspondence in reference to the Removal or Lighting of
DAUNT's ROCK, the Alteration or Improvement of ROCHE's LIGHT, the
providing of Fog Signals, and the better marking the Approaches to Cork
Harbour, from the 1st day of January 1865 to the 31st day of December
1873, between the Board of Trade, the Irish Lights Commissioners, the
Trinity Board, and the Cork Harbour Commissioners respectively : "

" And, of all Correspondence between the Board of Trade and the Liverpool Shipowners' and Steam Shipowners' Associations, and any other Public
Bodies and Private Shipping Firms, on the same Subjects."

Board of Trade,
21 April 1874.

T. H. FARRER.

(Mr. Murphy.)

Ordered, by The House of Commons, to be Printed,
22 April 1874.

CONTENTS.

PART I.

Correspondence between the Board of Trade and the Commissioners of Irish Lights, the Corporation of Trinity House, the Cork Harbour Commissioners, the Liverpool Shipowners' and Steam Shipowners' Association, and other Public Bodies and Private Shipping Firms - - - - - - - - 1

PART II.

Correspondence between the Commissioners of Irish Lights and the Corporation of Trinity House, and the Cork Harbour Commissioners (not included in Part I.)—[As returned by the Commissioners of Irish Lights] - - - 88

COPIES of all Correspondence in reference to the Removal or Lighting of
Daunt's Rock, the Alteration or Improvement of Roche's Light, the
providing of Fog Signals and the better marking the Approaches to Cork
Harbour from the 1st day of January 1865 to the 31st day of December
1873, between the Board of Trade, the Irish Lights Commissioners, the
Trinity Board, and the Cork Harbour Commissioners respectively :— And,
of all Correspondence between the Board of Trade and the Liverpool
Shipowners' and Steam Shipowners' Associations, and any other Public
Bodies and Private Shipping Firms, on the same Subjects.

Part I.

CORRESPONDENCE between the Board of Trade and the Commissioners of
Irish Lights, the Corporation of Trinity House, the Cork Harbour Commissioners, the Liverpool Shipowners' and Steam Shipowners' Associations,
and other Public Bodies and Private Shipping Firms.

— No. 1. —

Cork Harbour Commissioners to Board of Trade.

(H. 2786).

Cork Harbour Commissioners' Office. Cork,
8 January 1866.

Sir,
I am directed by the Cork Harbour Commissioners to forward you enclosed
copies of reports lately made on the additional light at Roche's Point.

I am. &c.

The Secretary,   (signed)   James F. Sugrue,
Marine Department, Board of Trade,   Secretary.
London.

Enclosure 1, in No. 1.

Report of H. H. O'Bryen, Harbour Master, Queenstown, upon Lights on Roche's Point.

I went off in the Commissioners' steam tug on Friday night the 29th December, and
again on Monday the 2nd January.
Friday night was clear and calm, Monday hazy ; the revolving light showed bright and
well, and in my opinion is a first-rate light.
Steamed off until the Old Head of Kinsale Light bore west by south, the bright light
marking Daunt's Rock, and exhibited from Roche's Point, shows to seaward between the
bearings of S.W. by W., and S.W. ½, or between Roberts' Head, and a distance of half a
mile to the eastward of Daunt's Rock.
This light in my opinion is a good guide in clear weather, but in thick or hazy weather
it would be likely to deceive, when outside the rock, as it blinds itself with the revolving
light, and its brightness makes the revolving light, when at its greatest brilliancy, look like
a flashing light; these may be mistaken for Ballycotton Light; again, it does not indicate
a ship's position, if she be north or south of the rock, which may be essential to her safety
if bound for Cork Harbour.
From what I could judge of the lights on both occasions, it is my opinion that, as now
placed, they are not sufficient to prevent ships from being wrecked upon Daunt's Rock.

0.67.   A 2   If

If allowed to suggest what would do away with all danger from this rock; first, if practicable, blow it away, if not, place a lightship to the south-east of it with a green light, or build a second lighthouse on Roche's Point, so that when both lights are in one, you may run for the harbour, keeping them so until you got to the entrance; they should be of different colours, say red, revolving as at present, the western light, and white the eastern light, so that when the revolving light was open to the westward of the white light, you are west of Daunt's Rock; when both lights in one sufficiently to the eastward, to run for the harbour; when revolving light opens east of white light, you would be well to the eastward of Daunt's Rock.

The fog bell cannot be heard more than a mile off in calm weather.

Enclosure 2, in No. 1.

Gentlemen,   Cork, 4 January 1865.

In pursuance of your directions to inspect and report upon the lights at Roche's Point, I beg to say that on the night of the 30th December, I proceeded to sea with Captain O'Bryen in the Commissioners' steam tug, the night being dark, but clear; that when about eight miles south-east of Cork Harbour, the revolving light at Roche's Point was distinctly visible, showing its maximum brilliancy for about six seconds in every minute, and I therefore consider it a good and sufficient seaward light, but am of opinion, that within the harbour from Roche's Point to the Spit, a fixed light would be a better guide for ships entering or leaving the harbour, particularly in thick or hazy weather.

With respect to the white light exhibited lower down on Roche's Tower, in order to guide ships clear of Daunt's Rock, I beg to say that though it is a good bright light, I do not consider it at present effective for that purpose. One objection that applies to all lights so near each other is, that when the observer is a long way off from them, they appear as one light, and this we found to be the case with these lights on Roche's Tower. But the principal objection is, that the white light is visible too far to the westward; so that a ship having passed the land a little too close may not see the light in bray weather till she was so near, that in attempting to haul out so as to bring the lights on her port bow, she might happen to encounter the very danger the light was meant to save her from. For every reason I think that in order to guide ships clear of Daunt's Rock, the proper place for a light would be on Roberts' Head, as it would at all times not only indicate the position of the rock, but the exact distance from Cork Harbour, and would be of the greatest advantage to all mariners navigating that part of the coast. As I need hardly remind you that the rock has now become so dangerous in consequence of the remains of the "City of New York" lying on it, that craft which might formerly have sailed over it at any time of tide with impunity, may now be wrecked on it even at high water, and, therefore, I consider the danger of so much importance, that I think it right to urge on your consideration the necessity for a light on Roberts' Head. At the same time, I may remark that if the Roche's Tower Light is to be retained for the purpose, it would be rendered more effective if so screened or obscured from view, that it could not be visible from Daunt's Rock, or any place to the westward of it.

I am, &c.
(signed)   Thomas C. Clarke,
                Harbour Master.

To the Cork Harbour Commissioners.

— No. 2. —

Board of Trade to Cork Harbour Commissioners.

(H. 2786.)

                              Board of Trade, Harbour Department,
Sir,   Whitehall, 19 January 1865.

I am directed by the Board of Trade to acknowledge the receipt of your letter of the 9th instant, relative to the additional light at Roche's Point, and, in reply, to inform you that the reports enclosed therein have been referred to the Port of Dublin Corporation.

I am also to observe, that the Roche's Point Light alone ought to be sufficient to ensure vessels passing Daunt Rock in safety. The second light was placed as an additional means of leading vessels to the eastward of the rock, and no attempt should be made to guide vessels by night between the rock and the shore, as it would be a most dangerous and improper course for any vessel to take.

I am, &c.
The Secretary,   (signed)   James Booth.
Cork Harbour Commissioners.

— No. 3. —

Board of Trade to Dublin Ballast Board.

(H. 2786.)

Board of Trade, Harbour Department,
Whitehall, 19 January 1864.

Sir,

I am directed by the Board of Trade to transmit to you, for the consideration of the Port of Dublin Corporation, two reports which have been received from the Cork Harbour Commissioners relative to the light at Roche's Point for marking Daunt Rock, and to request that you will be so good as to direct the attention of the Commissioners to the remarks respecting the blending of the second light with the revolving light.

As the reports are in original, I am to request that they may be returned.

I am, &c.
(signed)   James Booth.

The Secretary,
Ballast Office, Dublin.

— No. 4. —

Dublin Ballast Board to Board of Trade.

(H. 2903.)

Sir,

Ballast Office, Dublin, 29 January 1864.

Having submitted to the Board your letter of the 19th instant, No. H. 2786, transmitting two reports which their Lordships have received from the Cork Harbour Commissioners, relative to the light at " Roche's Point " for marking " Daunt Rock," I am directed to inform you similar documents had been forwarded to this Board, and that the Inspector of Lights is engaged in making necessary inquiries to enable him to report fully on the subject.

I am, &c.
(signed)   W. Lees, Secretary.

The Secretary, &c., &c.,
Marine Department.

— No. 5. —

Dublin Ballast Board to Board of Trade.

(H. 2994.)

Sir,

Ballast Office, Dublin, 6 February 1864.

With reference to previous correspondence on the subject, and to my letter of the 29th ultimo, I am directed to forward, for the consideration of the Privy Council for Trade, copy of a report approved of by the Board, from the Inspector of Lights, on the several communications referred to him (copies herewith), relative to the alteration in the " Roche's Point " light, and the better marking of the " Daunt Rock."

I am to add, copies of these documents have also been sent to the Trinity House.

I am, &c.
(signed)   W. Lees, Secretary.

The Secretary, &c., &c.,
Marine Department.

Enclosure 1, in No. 5.

Sir,   Ballast Office, Dublin, 27 January 1844.

I have read the letters referred to me by the Board, from the Cork Harbour Commissioners of the 9th and 18th instant, and their Enclosures, together with one from the Board of Trade on the same subject, dated the 19th instant, as well as one from Mr. Lake Joseph Shaw, relative to the lights at present on Roche's Point, at the entrance to Cork Harbour.

As there are so many conflicting opinions and suggestions expressed in these reports, it is desirable to comment on each separately.

CAPTAIN CLARKE'S REPORT.

First. He considers the revolving light to be a good and efficient seaward light, but is of opinion that within the harbour a fixed light would be a better guide for vessels entering or leaving it, particularly in thick or hazy weather.

On this I would observe, that as it appears from both the Cork Harbour-masters' reports this light is so superior when seen from seaward to the former fixed light (so frequently complained of), the slight loss in its efficiency as a guide within the harbour is more than counterbalanced by the advantage gained by the change.

Secondly. He does not consider the white light at present effective for the purpose of guiding vessels clear of the " Daunt Rock," because when observed a long way off both lights appear as one.

This objection appears to me groundless, as these lights, in clear weather, do not blend within eight miles of Roche's Point, which is five miles from the Daunt's Rock; and in hazy weather, should they appear to do so at a nearer distance, it would then be necessary to use caution, and not steer for them until they were brought on a safe bearing, which always had to be done before the white light was exhibited.

Another objection stated by him is, that vessels having hugged the land too close may not see the white light in hazy weather until so near, that in attempting to haul out they might encounter the very danger the light was intended to guard.

This objection is common to all lights under similar circumstances (when dangers are to seaward of the lights), and even a light placed on Roberts' Head as proposed by him, a vessel in thick weather, seeing it suddenly, might, from the uncertainty of her position, consider it necessary either to haul off from it, or to slack it and run the same risk that Captain Clarke complains of.

His suggestion to alter the light, so that it might not be seen from Daunt's Rock or to the westward of it, amounts to the same changing it from a danger light, as at present (to be avoided), to a fair way light (to be kept in view), and I do not see that any advantage would be gained by such change.

CAPTAIN O'BRYEN'S REPORT.

First. He considers the white light a good guide in clear weather, but in thick or hazy weather it would be likely to deceive when outside the rock, as it blends with the revolving light, and its brightness makes the revolving light, when at its greatest brilliancy, look like a fixed or leading light, and may be mistaken for the Ballycotton Light.

I have already observed that the two lights do not blend in clear weather within eight miles from Roche's Point, which is five miles outside the rock, and this is corroborated by Captain Clarke's letter accompanying (the vertical distance between the lights being so great); and in hazy weather, should they appear to do so at a nearer distance, caution should be observed on approaching, as I have before stated, in dealing with Captain Clarke's Report. Neither do I think they are likely to be mistaken for Ballycotton (even supposing they were seen at that distance in thick weather), as there is such a marked difference between the period of revolution in these lights, Ballycotton flashing every 10 seconds, " Roche's Point" revolving once every minute.

Secondly. He suggests either the blowing away of the rock or placing a lightship south east of it, or erecting a second lighthouse on Roche's Point.

No doubt the first would be the most effectual remedy, the practicability of which is a question for an engineer to decide.

A lightship placed south east of the rock would be a good guide to clear this danger so long as it was visible, but for the safety of her crew it would be necessary to place her one mile and a quarter from the rock; and in thick weather the light might not be seen at that distance, therefore the Bell Boat Buoy the Board is about to place there will be much more effective under these circumstances.

The erecting of a second lighthouse on Roche's Point would not answer the purpose expressed by him, there not being space at the point to admit of their being placed sufficiently apart, in order to make such an arrangement fully effective.

In

In reference to the complaints signed by the masters of steamers sailing out of the port of Cork, I think them well deserving of the attention of the Board, for the Harbour Rock being off of Roche's Point obliges vessels running in for the harbour to hug the point closer than would be otherwise necessary in order to avoid it, and with a following sea a vessel is very likely to yaw considerably, and this might happen when close to the point, and the light at the same time in its revolution eclipsed, when the helmsman losing sight of it would have nothing to guide him in checking her yawing except the compass, which might not act sufficiently quick at this critical moment when so close to the danger.

I therefore recommend that their suggestion (to make the time of the illumination longer and that of the eclipse shorter) should be carried out, which can be done without altering the present period of revolution.

Mr. Shaw's recommendation of placing a light on Roberts' Head has already been remarked on in this report.

I am, &c.

The Secretary,
Port of Dublin Corporation.

(signed)   E. F. Roberts,
Inspector of Lights.

Enclosure 2, in No. 5.

Cork Harbour Commissioners' Office,
Cork, 23 January 1865.

Sir,

In answer to yours of the 21st instant, I beg to say that when I perceived the lights on Roche's Point to blend, we were about one mile S.W. ¼ W. of the lights.

Yours, &c.

W. Lees, Esq.,
Secretary, Ballast Office, Dublin.

(signed)   Thomas C. Clarke,
Harbour Master.

Enclosure 3, in No. 5.

Cork Harbour Commissioners' Office,
Queenstown, 17 January 1865.

Sir,

In reply to your favour of the 21st instant, No. 184, which should have been replied to sooner, were it not that I have been much engaged.

The light, in my opinion, blends itself into the revolving light in hazy weather at or near the Rock, and does not show sufficiently to the eastward to be a sure guide in any weather.

The revolving light is too long obscured for a harbour light.

I am, &c.

W. Lees, Esq.,
Secretary, Ballast Office, Dublin.

(signed)   H. H. O'Bryen.

Enclosure 4, in No. 5.

Cork Harbour Commissioners' Office,
Cork, 6 January 1866.

Sir,

By directions of the Cork Harbour Commissioners, I beg to enclose you copies of reports lately made on the additional light at Roche's Point; as also to inquire when the beacon, as recommended by the Board of Trade, will be put on Daunt's Rock.

I am, &c.

W. Lees, Esq.,
Secretary, Ballast Board, Dublin.

(signed)   James F. Seymour,
Secretary.

Enclosure 5, in No. 5.

(Similar to Enclosure 2, in No. 1.)

Enclosure 6, in No. 5.

(Similar to Enclosure 1, in No. 1.)

Enclosure 7, in No. 5.

Cork Harbour Commissioners' Office, Cork,
12 January 1866.

Sir,

Both your favours of the 13th and 15th are to hand. I now beg to enclose copies of two communications lately addressed to this board; and am,

Yours, &c.

W. Lees, Esq.,
Ballast Board, Dublin.

(signed)   James F. Sugrue,
Secretary.

Enclosure 8, in No. 5.

Steamer "Apollo," 6 January 1865.

Sir,

Since the Roche's Point Light has been altered from a fixed into a revolving light, and the time from the shade to the showing bright again to seaward, it is dangerous to make the harbour, more particularly in hazy or foggy weather. It is too long revolving for a second bearing before she would be in a dangerous position. On two voyages I have been so situated by the length of time the light is revolving, and as far as my experience goes (20 years at sea), a worse alteration from a fixed light to a revolving for a harbour light there could not be. It would have been a great boon had the old fixed light been reflected larger. I fear accidents will occur should the light remain as it is. I take the liberty of placing this before the Cork Harbour Board through you, as Harbour Commissioner, representing the Bristol Steam Navigation Company here.

I am, &c.

To Ebenezer Pike, Esq.

(signed)   James Poole, R.N.

Enclosure 9, in No. 5.

Cork, 11 January 1865.

Gentlemen,

At a meeting of your board, held on Wednesday the 4th instant, your harbour-masters, Captains O'Bryen and Clarke, sent in reports approving of the revolving light on Roche's Point, as a good and efficient light for the harbour.

We regret being obliged to differ from both these gentlemen, as we consider it a very unsafe and dangerous description of light to run for as a harbour light on a thick or hazy night with a gale blowing on the coast. When running in for the harbour in thick or hazy weather, blowing hard on the coast, there is generally a heavy sea, and this light, under these circumstances, is the principal guide the master of a ship has to depend on, as, owing to the heave of the sea when approaching the entrance of the harbour, a ship is thrown off her course a couple of points very quickly, but with a steady object in view (a fixed light) the ship's proper course is quickly recovered, and there is no fear of getting on shore. The present revolving light, under similar circumstances, could only be seen for a few seconds once in a minute, and if not clear just at the time it revolves they must take all their luck and look out for the next revolution, or perhaps the succeeding one; and when seen it is visible for so short a time that it is impossible it can be of much service to steer by unless to indicate to the master that he is off the harbour. In the event of your deciding on retaining a revolving light, we would respectfully suggest that the period of illumination and eclipse be reversed, and that its maximum brilliancy be 50 seconds instead of six, as at present, so as to allow it to approach as near as possible to a fixed light, similar to that which was recently removed, or, more efficient still, the adoption of the two lighthouses, as recommended by Captain Tooker in his letter of the 18th January 1864, and also in Captain O'Bryen's Report to the Commissioners on last board day.

Feeling it incumbent on us to place these our views before your board,

We are, &c.

(signed)   S. S. Meale, "Halcyon."
James Poole, Lieutenant, R.N.
Thomas Perry, "Osprey."
E. Byrne, "P. Adler."
S. Berridge, "Bittern."
Thos. Brumfller, "Pelican."
Stephen Anderson, "Tusker."
Robert Stanely, "Sabrine."
Francis J. Croft, "Cormorant."
Henry Le Bayeux, "Dodo."

The Cork Harbour Commissioners.

DAUNT'S ROCK (CORK HARBOUR).

— No. 6. —

Board of Trade to Dublin Ballast Board.

(H. 2994.)

Board of Trade, Harbour Department,
Whitehall, 10 February 1866.

Sir,

I am directed by the Board of Trade to acknowledge the receipt of your letter of the 6th instant, transmitting a copy of the Report of the Inspector of Lights relative to marking Daunt's Rock, and in reply to acquaint you, for the information of the Port of Dublin Corporation, that the Board of Trade concur in the opinions expressed by Captain Roberts; and with reference to the alteration in Roche's Point Light, think it desirable to increase the period during which the light is seen without altering the period of revolution; and I am to request that an estimate of the cost of the work may be furnished.

The Secretary,
Ballast Office, Dublin.

(signed)   T. H. Farrer.

— No. 7. —

Dublin Ballast Board to Board of Trade.

(H. 3217.)

Sir,

Ballast Office, Dublin, 24 February 1866.

Having submitted to the Board your letter of the 10th instant (No. H. 2994), stating the Privy Council for Trade concur in the opinions expressed by Captain Roberts in his report transmitted on the 6th instant, and requesting to be furnished with an estimate of the cost of the work in carrying out the proposed alteration in Roche's Point Light.

I am, in reply, directed to forward the estimate as submitted by the Inspector of Lights, and to state this Board is now making arrangements to carry out the change alluded to.

The Secretary, &c. &c.
Marine Department.

(signed)   W. Lees,
Secretary.

Enclosure in No. 7.

Sir,

Ballast Office, Dublin, 23 February 1866.

I beg to report to the Board that the expense for changing the present revolving light at Roche's Point (by increasing the period of illumination, but without altering the time of revolution) will amount altogether (including travelling expenses) to about 45 £. sterling.

I am, &c.

(signed)   E. F. Roberts,
Inspector of Lights.

The Secretary,
Port of Dublin Corporation.

— No. 8. —

Board of Trade to Dublin Ballast Board.

(H. 3217.)

Sir,

Board of Trade, Harbour Department,
Whitehall, 1 March 1866.

I am directed by the Board of Trade to acknowledge the receipt of your letter of the 24th ult. relative to Roche's Point Light, and in reply to acquaint you, for the information of the Port of Dublin Corporation, that the Board of Trade approves of the expenditure of a sum not exceeding 45 £. for effecting the desired alteration in the period of revolution of the light.

I am, &c.

(signed)   T. H. Farrer.

The Secretary,
Ballast Office, Dublin.

— No. 9. —

Mr. Inman to Board of Trade.

(H. 3999.)

Liverpool, New York, and Philadelphia
Steamship Company,
Liverpool, 31 May 1865.

My Lords,

I have the honour to address your Lordships on the subject of Daunt's Rock, and to draw your attention to the fact that no warning has been placed there further than the common buoy which was near it when this Company's steamer, "City of New York," was lost on it in March 1864.

This Company's steamer, "City of London," with 141 cabin, 806 steerage passengers, and 106 crew, (altogether 853 souls), on board, was almost within her own length of the same danger on Tuesday the 23rd instant, which would not have occurred had even a second common buoy been placed in the position which I pointed out to your Lordships last year, as the safe, and in our opinion, proper point for vessels approaching from America.

The circumstances were as follows: The "City of London" had landed her despatches at Cape Clear at 6 a.m., and while proceeding the remaining 50 miles to Queenstown she became enveloped in dense fog about 8 a.m. The engines were repeatedly stopped, constantly slowed, and soundings frequently taken, with hand and deep sea leads, at last at 0.50 p.m. a sounding of 14 fathoms being taken, the anchor was instantly let go, watches were posted both on deck and (the second officer) at the fore topmast head, but nothing whatever could be seen. At 1.30 p.m. the fog lifted, showing Daunt's Rock buoy (in the Captain's report) "little more than 100 yards from me, bearing N. E. ½ N., right in a line with Roche's Point, the buoy one point abaft the beam, and Robert's Head right astern."

The fact was that the vessel was anchored between Daunt's Rock buoy and Daunt's Rock, with her stern hanging almost close to Daunt's Rock, with nothing whatever to intimate her danger.

The value of the vessel, specie and cargo, was nearly a quarter of a million sterling, besides the passengers and the full mails.

I trust we shall not again have to appeal in vain for some efficient steps to be taken to mark this highly dangerous spot.

I have, &c.

(signed) William Inman.

To the Right Honourable
The Lords of Her Majesty's Privy Council
for Trade and Plantations, London.

— No. 10. —

Board of Trade to Mr. W. Inman.

(H. 3999.)

Board of Trade, Harbour Department,
Whitehall, 9 June 1865.

Sir,

I am directed by the Board of Trade to acknowledge the receipt of your letter of the 31st ultimo, complaining that there is not an efficient fog signal to warn vessels off Daunt Rock, and, in reply, to acquaint you that the Board of Trade gave their sanction to the placing of a good bell-boat to mark Daunt Rock in September last.

It appears to the Board of Trade, as at present advised, that the danger threatened to the "City of London" steamer arose not so much from a deficiency of a good fog signal at Daunt Rock, as from the vessel using hauled in shore during the prevalence of a fog so dense as to render objects invisible even at a few yards' distance, and from disregarding the warning which more frequent soundings would have given of the vessel's approach to danger.

— No. 11. —

Board of Trade to Dublin Ballast Board.

(H. 3999.)

Board of Trade, Harbour Department,
Whitehall, 9 June 1845.

Sir,
I am directed by the Board of Trade to transmit to you, for the information
of the Port of Dublin Corporation, the enclosed copy of a letter from Mr. Inman,
and to request that they may be informed when the new bell buoy is to be
placed at Daunt's Rock.

I am, &c.

The Secretary, Ballast Office, Dublin.   (signed)   T. H. Farrer.

— No. 12. —

Dublin Ballast Board to Board of Trade.

(H. 4089.)

Sir,   Ballast Office, Dublin, 15 June 1845.
With reference to your letter of the 9th instant (H. 3999), I am directed to
acquaint you, for the information of their Lordships, that the bell boat was
placed off Daunt's Rock on the 10th instant, as will be seen by the accompanying
report from the Inspector of Lights, and that the Board have approved of
Captain Roberts' suggestion to retain the original buoy in its position.

I am, &c.

The Secretary,   (signed)   W. Lees, Secretary.
Marine Department, Board of Trade.

Enclosure in No. 12.

Sir,   Ballast Office, Dublin, 14 June 1845.
I beg to report to the Board that Mr. Graham H. Hills, having on his final examination
of the Bell Boat Buoy, approved of her construction and passed her; I received her from
the contractors, Messrs. Walpole, Webb, & Bewley, on Friday last, the 9th instant, and
proceeded with her to the Daunt Rock in tow of the " Princess Alexandra " steamer, and
arrived at 5 p.m. the following day, and placed the Bell Boat Buoy in position, viz., 120
fathoms south-south-west of the rock, leaving the former buoy still marking the east side
of the rock ; and I consider now, with both these marks, that the Daunt Rock is efficiently
guarded.

The day I placed the buoy was remarkably calm, not a ripple on the water, which pre-
vented my having an opportunity of judging of its effect, but should I find with a swell
on that the buoy is too sluggish in its movements, I would recommend the removal of a
a portion of her ballast.

I am, &c.

The Secretary,   (signed)   E. F. Roberts,
Port Dublin Corporation.   Inspector of Lights.

— No. 18. —

Commissioners of Irish Lights* to Board of Trade.

(H. 3776 a.)   Irish Lights Office, Westmoreland-street,
Sir,   Dublin, 12 November 1867.

I am directed to forward herewith, for the consideration of the Lords of the
Committee of Privy Council for Trade, copies of communications addressed to
the Commissioners by Captain Palmer, stating he is prepared to enter into a
contract for cutting down the "Daunt" Rock, near Cork Harbour, to a level
of five fathoms below low water; and that he estimates the cost for the work
will be from, say, 6,000l. to 8,000l., on the understanding, however, that no
money is required on account or otherwise, until the work is completed.

The Assistant Secretary, &c., &c.,   (signed)   W. Lees, Secretary.
Harbour Department, Board of Trade.   I am, &c.

Enclosure 1, in No. 18.

                                Terminus Hotel, London Bridge, London,
Sir,   29 October 1867.

Some time since, when the steamship "City of New York" was wrecked on the Daunt's
Rock, at the suggestion of Mr. Maguire, the then Mayor of Cork, I made a survey of the
rock, and also to estimate of the cost of cutting it down to a level of five fathoms below
low water.

Since then I have perfected some machinery, and am now prepared to make your Board
(or such person as would entertain it) an offer to take a contract for the removal of the top
to the depth above mentioned, on terms so very low and moderate that I think there would
be no longer any objection to have the work done.

I am, of course, willing to bear every risk and expense, and to agree that no charge
whatever shall be made until the work has been performed to the satisfaction of your
Board; on these terms it has occurred to me that perhaps a contract might be granted,
especially as, if I fail to do what I am confident I can accomplish, no harm could possibly
be done to any one but myself.

I have therefore to request you will kindly let me know if there is any chance of obtaining
a contract if my terms are suitable. I do not of course ask you to promise anything, but if
you give me any hopes I will at once come over.

Waiting favour of your esteemed reply,

The Secretary, Ballast Board.   (signed)   Hugh Palmer.
                                             I am, &c.

Enclosure 2, in No. 18.

                                Terminus Hotel, London Bridge, London,
Sir,   4 November 1867.

In reply to your esteemed letter of the 2nd instant, requiring an approximate estimate of
the cost of removing the top of this rock, so as to leave water to the depth of five fathoms
at low water over the remaining portion of the rock, I beg to say that I am endeavouring
to obtain a contract for the removal of the Swilley Rocks in the Menai Straits, and if I
obtain it I could make a lower estimate for the Daunt's Bank; but for your present
guidance, I may say that the cost will be from six to eight thousand pounds (say 6,000l. to
8,000l.), but on the understanding that no money is required on account or otherwise,
until the work is completed to the satisfaction of your Board.

Waiting the favour of your esteemed reply,

The Secretary, Ballast Board, Dublin.   (signed)   Hugh Palmer.
                                             I am, &c.

---

* The name of the General Lighthouse Authority in Ireland was on the 17th June 1867 (30 Vict.
c. lxxxi), changed to "The Commissioners of Irish Lights."

— No. 14. —

Board of Trade to Commissioners of Irish Lights.

(H. 3776 a.)

Board of Trade, Harbour Department,
Whitehall, 16 November 1887.

Sir,

I am directed by the Board of Trade to acknowledge the receipt of your letter of the 12th instant, transmitting copies of communications from Mr. Palmer, which state that he is prepared to remove the Daunt Rock near Cork Harbour, so as to leave water to the depth of five fathoms at low water over the remaining portion of the rock; and, in reply, I am to request that you will move the Commissioners to ascertain, for the information of this Board, what experience Mr. Palmer has already had in the removal of sub-marine rocks, and also whether he would be willing to allow an engineer named by this Board to judge of the feasibility of his plan.

I am, &c.
(signed) C. Cecil Trevor.

The Secretary.
Commissioners of Irish Lights.

— No. 15. —

Board of Trade to Commissioners of Irish Lights.

(H. 4270.)

Board of Trade, Harbour Department,
Whitehall, 27 December 1887.

Sir,

With reference to your letter of the 16th November, relative to Mr. Hugh Palmer's application to be employed in cutting down the Daunt Rock near Cork Harbour, I am directed by the Board of Trade to acquaint you, for the information of the Irish Lights Commissioners, that Mr. Palmer had made a similar application to them with regard to the Scilly Rocks in the Menai Straits; as Mr. Palmer appeared desirous of explaining the process by which he proposed to carry out these works to some competent engineer, the Board of Trade, with the sanction of the Elder Brethren, referred him to Mr. Douglass, the engineer to the Trinity House, a copy of whose report is enclosed for the information of the Commissioners of Irish Lights.

I am to add that should the Commissioners of Irish Lights feel disposed to try the experiment with respect to Daunt's Rock, it will be for them to make proposals as to the agreement with Mr. Palmer.

I am, &c.
(signed) C. Cecil Trevor.

The Secretary,
Commissioners of Irish Lights.

Enclosure in No. 15.

Mr. Palmer proposes to drill holes in the rocks to be operated upon, charge them with powder, or nitro-glycerine, and blast in the usual manner; but, for the purpose of drilling the blast holes rapidly and economically, he proposes to use rock-drilling machinery; this machinery to be placed in position on the rock by a diver, and to be worked by compressed air supplied through a flexible tube from suitable air-compressing machinery, worked by a steam-engine as on board a vessel moored over the rock.

The rock-drilling machinery proposed to be used by Mr. Palmer is that designed by Harman Reeves, civil engineer, United States of America. This machinery was exhibited at the Paris Exhibition; it is light, portable, and compact, and is reported to have worked very satisfactorily on tunnelling works in America.

I am of opinion that the plan proposed by Mr. Palmer for using rock-drilling machinery for sub-marine blasting operations is quite feasible for any situation where diving can be carried on.

P. R. Bevilton, Esq.   (signed)   J. N. Douglas.
&c. &c. &c.

— No. 16. —

Commissioners of Irish Lights to Board of Trade.

(H. 169.)

Irish Lights Office, Westmoreland-street,
Dublin, 18 January 1868.

Sir,

With reference to your letter of the 27th ultimo, H. 4370, I am directed to forward, for the instructions of their Lordships, copy of a communication from Mr. Palmer agreeing to enter into a contract for the removal of portion of the "Daunt" Rock, for the sum of eight thousand pounds (8,000 l.) on the conditions named in previous correspondence.

I am to state the deputation who recently had an interview in London with Mr. Palmer were informed by that gentleman that he would execute this work for seven thousand pounds (7,000 l.); and they were further led to believe that should he be so successful in obtaining a contract for the removal of the Swilly Rocks, Menai Straits, for which he was in treaty with the Trinity House, he would be prepared to perform the work for a lower sum.

The Board would therefore suggest that inquiry be made whether the Elder Brethren have accepted Mr. Palmer's offer, and should such be the case the Board would then be in a position to offer, with their Lordships' sanction, Mr. Palmer's seven thousand pounds for the execution of the work.

I am to express the strong opinion of the Board as to the desirability of removing this danger, an opinion they are further strengthened in, bearing in mind the recent accident to H. M. sloop "Research."

I am, &c.

The Assistant Secretary,   (signed)   W. Lees, Secretary.
&c., &c.,
Harbour Department, Board of Trade.

Enclosure in No. 16.

North British Hotel, Glasgow,
6 January 1868.

Sir,

In reply to your favour of the 3rd instant, I beg to state that I am quite willing to enter into a contract for the removal of the portion of the "Daunt's Rock" upon the terms already stated by me in former letters, for the sum of 8,000 l., such sum to be paid on completion of the work to the satisfaction of your Board; and would suggest that you instruct your solicitor to make out a draft contract on that basis, and I will immediately return it with any alterations that may be required.

I am, &c.

The Secretary, Ballast Board, Dublin.   (signed)   Hugh Palmer.

— No. 17. —

Board of Trade to Commissioners of Irish Lights.

(H. 169.)

Board of Trade, Harbour Department,
Whitehall, 17 January 1862.

Sir,

I am directed by the Board of Trade to acknowledge the receipt of your letter of the 13th instant, transmitting an offer from Mr. Palmer to remove a portion of the Daunt Rock for the sum of 8,000 *l.*, and in reply to acquaint you, for the information of the Commissioners of Irish Lights, that, in the opinion of this Board, further inquiry should be made into Mr. Palmer's antecedents before a work of this importance is entrusted to him.

I am, &c.
(signed) C. Cecil Trevor.

The Secretary,
Commissioners of Irish Lights.

— No. 18. —

Commissioners of Irish Lights to Board of Trade.

(H. 823.)

Irish Lights Office, Westmoreland-street,
Dublin, 25 February 1862.

Sir,

With reference to your letter of the 17th ultimo, H. 169, relative to an offer from Captain Palmer to remove a portion of "Daunt's Rock," and requesting that their Lordships may be informed, on inquiry by the Commissioners of Irish Lights, what experience Captain Palmer has had in the removal of submarine rocks, I am directed to forward herewith copy of a letter from that gentleman, affording the required information.

I am, &c.
(signed) W. Lees,
Secretary.

The Assistant Secretary,
Harbour Department, Board of Trade.

Enclosure in No. 18.

Hôtel de l'Europe, Antwerp,
22 February 1862.

Sir,

I have to acknowledge receipt of your esteemed favour of the 21st instant, and in reply beg to state that I am quite prepared to accept the contract on the terms of my former letters, and of course expect no payment until the work is finished to your satisfaction.

In reply to the question as to my past experience, I would repeat what I have already said. I have had some slight experience in blasting rocks under water, but great experience in general sub-marine engineering, and in mining and quarry work on land.

I remain, &c.
(signed) Hugh Palmer,
Captain, R. M. S.

W. Lees, Esq., &c. &c.

— No. 19 —

Board of Trade to Commissioners of Irish Lights.

(H. 823.)

Board of Trade, Harbour Department,
Whitehall, 6 March 1862.

Sir,

I am directed by the Board of Trade to acknowledge the receipt of your letter of the 25th ultimo on the subject of the offer which has been made by Mr. Palmer to remove a portion of Daunt's Rock, and transmitting copy of a letter from him relating to the experience which he states he has had in the removal of sub-marine rocks.

In

0.67. c 3

In reply, I am to request that you will state to the Commissioners that, in the opinion of the Board of Trade, it would be undesirable to accept the services of Mr. Palmer.

The Secretary,
Commissioners of Irish Lights.

I am, &c.
(signed)   C. Cecil Trevor.

— No. 20. —

Commissioners of Irish Lights to Board of Trade.

(H. 1111.)

Irish Lights Office, Westmoreland-street,
Dublin, 14 March 1896.

Sir,

With reference to your letter of the 6th instant (H. 893), acknowledging my letter of 24th ultimo on the subject of Captain Palmer's offer to remove a portion of the Daunt Rock, their Lordships stating they were of opinion it would be undesirable to accept his services, I am to state, having submitted your letter to the Commissioners at their meeting on Friday week last, they passed a resolution "that Captain Palmer be informed the Board of Trade will not sanction the expenditure."

A letter from Captain Palmer having been subsequently received, and before the order of the Commissioners had been carried out, I beg to enclose a copy of same, this letter being in reply to a communication addressed to him on the 2nd instant, copy herewith, stating the Commissioners were prepared to recommend the Board of Trade to sanction his being given the contract on the terms named in his letters, provided he gives satisfactory references as to his capacity to perform the proposed work.

I have the honour, therefore, to request your further instructions.

I am, &c.
(signed)   W. Lees,
Secretary.

The Assistant Secretary,
Harbour Department, Board of Trade.

Enclosure 1, in No. 20.

Sir,

Irish Lights Office, Dublin, 2 March 1896.

I am to acknowledge your further letter of the 23rd ultimo, and am to inform you the Commissioners are prepared to recommend the Board of Trade to sanction your being given the contract for the removal of portion of Daunt's Rock on the terms named in your letter, provided you give them satisfactory references as to your capacity to perform the proposed work.

Captain Palmer, &c. &c., Antwerp.

I am, &c.
(signed)   W. Lees, Secretary.

Enclosure 2, in No. 20.

Sir,

Tavistock Hotel, London, 4 March 1896.

I have to acknowledge receipt of your esteemed favour of the 2nd instant, in which you ask me to give satisfactory references as to my capacity to perform the proposed work.

I have some time since replied to your inquiries on this subject, and at your request submitted my plans to your engineer, Mr. Douglas, as well as to the deputation that called upon me at my hotel last December. In a previous letter you stated that your Board had received a satisfactory report.

Considering that I am willing to invest several thousand pounds in this contract, and that I have never asked for or expected any sort of assistance from your Board, I am at a loss to understand how "my capacity to perform the proposed work" can be a matter of

moment to anyone but myself. I have no desire to keep the contract to myself for any
indefinite time: you will soon see if I am capable or not.

If you will, however, let me know what information you require of my reference, I will do
my best to satisfy you upon the subject.

The Secretary, Irish Lights Office.

I remain, &c.
(signed) *Hugh Palmer.*

— No. 21. —

Board of Trade to Commissioners of Irish Lights.

(H. 1011.)

Board of Trade, Harbour Department,
Whitehall, 30 March 1866.

Sir,

WITH reference to your letter of the 14th instant, and previous correspondence
on the subject of Mr. Palmer's offer to remove a portion of the Daunt Rock, I
am directed by the Board of Trade to inform you, for the information of the
Commissioners of Irish Lights, that they are of opinion that the expenses relating
to the Rock ought not to be charged on the general trade, and that they consequently cannot authorise any expenditure out of the Mercantile Marine Fund
for the purpose of its removal, unless that fund is indemnified by a special toll
on the trade of Cork; and, considering the strong opinion expressed by the
trade of Cork in the year 1864 against their defraying the expenses of marking
Daunt's Rock, the Board of Trade, even if satisfied with Mr. Palmer's plan,
would feel a difficulty in authorising a charge for the purpose of paying Mr.
Palmer to be raised by a special tax on the trade of Cork, unless the Commissioners could obtain from those who represent that trade, some intimation of a
change of the opinion they formerly expressed.

If the local trade are prepared to pay, provided Mr. Palmer succeeds, or if it
should appear that the Post Office, having regard to the usefulness of Cork as a
mail station, are willing to provide the requisite funds, the Board of Trade see
no reason why the experiment should not be made, provided that no money is
advanced or promised to Mr. Palmer until the work has been accomplished to
the satisfaction of the Commissioners of Irish Lights.

The Secretary,
Commissioners of Irish Lights.

I am, &c.
(signed) *T. H. Farrer.*

— No. 22. —

Commissioners of Irish Lights to Board of Trade.

(H. 1579.)

Irish Lights Office, Westmoreland-street,
Dublin, 22 April 1866.

Sir,

WITH reference to your letter of the 30th ultimo (H. 1111), on subject of the
correspondence which has taken place relative to Mr. Palmer's offer to remove
a portion of the Daunt's Rock, off entrance to Cork Harbour, I am directed to
state that, acting on the suggestion of their Lordships, the Commissioners of
Irish Lights communicated with Her Majesty's Postmaster General and with
the Cork Harbour Board; and I am now to forward, for the information and
further instructions of the Lords of the Committee of Privy Council for Trade,
copy of the replies received from the respective parties.

The Assistant Secretary,
&c., &c.,
Harbour Department, Board of Trade.

I am, &c.
(signed) *W. Lees, Secretary.*

Enclosures in No. 22.

Harbour Commissioners' Office, Cork,
8 April 1868.

Sir,

I have the honour to acknowledge the receipt of your communication dated 20th ultimo, stating that the Commissioners of Irish Lights for some past have been in communication with the Board of Trade upon the subject of an offer for the removal of such a portion of "Daunt's Rock" as is at present dangerous to navigation, and that their Lordships express an opinion that if the attempt be made and prove successful, that the Port of Cork and Post Office authorities should contribute towards the expense.

I am directed by the Cork Harbour Commissioners to inform you that, as "Daunt's Rock" is outside the jurisdiction of this Board, they would not be justified in contributing towards its removal, and must therefore respectfully decline doing so.

I am, &c.
(signed) *William Dowsern,*
Secretary.

The Secretary, Ballast Board.

General Post Office, London,
9 April 1868.

Sir,

Having laid before the Postmaster General your letter of the 8th instant, enclosing a copy of a letter from the Board of Trade relative to an offer from Captain Hugh Palmer to remove the upper portion of "Daunt's Rock" off Cork Harbour, and inquiring whether this Department is willing to provide the requisite funds for this purpose, I am directed by His Grace to state that, as far as the Mail Packet Service is concerned, the question is one rather for the consideration of the contractors for the packets than of the Post Office.

I am, &c.
(signed) F. Hill

The Secretary, Irish Lights Office.

— No. 23. —

Board of Trade to Commissioners of Irish Lights.

(H. 1905.)

Board of Trade, Harbour Department,
Whitehall, 22 May 1868.

Sir,

With reference to your letter of the 22nd ultimo, transmitting copies of letters from the Postmaster General and the Cork Harbour Board, declining to contribute towards the expense of allowing Mr. Hugh Palmer to attempt to remove a portion of Daunt's Rock, I am directed by the Board of Trade to acquaint you, for the information of the Commissioners of Irish Lights, that they are prepared to receive, through the Elder Brethren of the Trinity House, a proposal to carry out the desired object on the following conditions :—

1. That no money whatever is to be paid to Mr. Palmer unless the work is successfully performed to the satisfaction of the Commissioners of Irish Lights.

2. That necessary precautions are taken, and that Mr. Palmer should agree to deposit his explosive materials in such a place as the police authorities of the district may consider safe.

3. That whatever sum of money may be paid out of the Mercantile Marine Fund for the purpose, an equivalent shall be paid by a special toll levied on the trade of Cork, so as to indemnify the Mercantile Marine Fund.

I am further to suggest that the Commissioners, in the event of their deciding to make such a proposal, should give the Cork authorities full and ample notice thereof, in order that the local trade may have the opportunity, should they desire, of objecting, before any contract is made with Mr. Palmer.

I am, &c.
(signed) C. Cecil Trevor.

The Secretary,
Commissioners of Irish Lights.

— No. 24. —

Commissioners of Irish Lights to Board of Trade.

(H. 2308.)

Irish Lights Office, Westmoreland-street,
Dublin, 15 June 1868.

Sir,

WITH reference to your further letter of the 22nd ultimo (H. 1903), on subject of the Postmaster General and the Cork Harbour Commissioners declining to contribute towards the expense of allowing Mr. Palmer to attempt to remove a portion of the Daunt's Rock, the Board of Trade stating they are now prepared to receive a proposal through the Elder Brethren of the Trinity House to carry out the desired object on conditions set forth in your communication, I am directed to acquaint you, this Board having forwarded to the Cork Harbour Commissioners copy of your letter, they have received a reply from that body, stating that as Daunt's Rock is outside their jurisdiction, they shall feel bound to resist any toll being on the trade of Cork for the furtherance of the above object.

I am to enclose copy of this reply, and to request you will be so good as to submit same for the consideration of their Lordships.

I am, &c.
(signed) W. Lees, Secretary.

The Assistant Secretary,
&c. &c.
Harbour Department, Board of Trade.

Enclosure in No. 24.

Harbour Commissioners' Office, Lapp's Quay, Cork,
6 June 1868.

Sir,

I HAVE the honour to acknowledge the receipt of your communication dated 1st instant, and its enclosure bearing date 22nd ultimo, relative to the removal of a portion of "Daunt's Rock," and stating that any sum of money which may be advanced for that purpose by the Mercantile Marine Board, should be secured by a toll levied on the trade of Cork.

I am directed by the Cork Harbour Commissioners to inform you that, "Daunt's Rock" being outside their jurisdiction, they shall feel bound to resist any toll being levied on the trade of Cork in furtherance of that object.

I am, &c.
(signed) William Donegan, Secretary.

The Secretary,
Commissioners of Irish Lights.

— No. 25. —

War Office to Board of Trade.

(H. 2328.)

War Office, 16 June 1868.

Sir,

I AM directed by the Secretary of State for War to acknowledge the receipt of your communication of the 13th ultimo (H. 1414), forwarding for his consideration copy of a report made by Mr. Douglass, Engineer to the Trinity Board, upon a proposal by Captain Palmer to remove the Swilly Rocks in the Menai Straits; and requesting that a report might be obtained as to Captain Palmer's proposal to remove the Daunt's Rock, at the entrance to Cork Harbour.

In reference to the latter subject I am to acquaint you, for the information of the Board of Trade, that the subject has been referred to the Director of the Royal Engineer establishment at Chatham; and to enclose a copy of that officer's report thereon for their consideration.

I am to request that you will move the Board to acquaint Sir John Pakington whether they would desire the survey, &c., suggested in the report enclosed, to be made; and whether they will provide the requisite funds for the same.

I have, &c.
(signed) Longford.

The Secretary, Board of Trade.

Encl. in No. 14.

Enclosure in No. 25.

Copy of Report from Director, Royal Engineer Establishment.

It is impossible, with the knowledge at present possessed of the effects of explosion of gunpowder and other explosive agents under water, to estimate the expense of removing the Daunt's Rock, or whether it will be advisable, with a view to economy, to use the boring machinery devised by Mr. Herman Haupt, as recommended by Mr. Palmer.

With a view to forming an opinion on this point, it would be advisable to have a careful survey made of the Rock and of its geological formation, and possibly to try the effect of some experimental charges.

With this view, I would recommend that an officer, with a party at per margin, be sent with diving apparatus, which can be lent from this establishment, to examine the rock in question.

Of course I presume that an appropriate vessel would be provided for the purpose.

The expense of this examination would only amount to the working pay of the party, and probably a few small charges of powder for experiments.

— No. 25 A. —

Board of Trade to Commissioners of Irish Lights.

(H. 2308.)

Board of Trade, Harbour Department.
Whitehall Gardens, 28 June 1868.

Sir,

I am directed by the Board of Trade to acknowledge the receipt of your letter of the 18th instant, transmitting copy of a letter from the Cork Harbour Commissioners, stating that the Daunt's Rock being out of their jurisdiction they should feel bound to resist any toll being levied on the trade of Cork in furtherance of the removal of the rock.

In reply I am to acquaint you, for the information of the Commissioners of Irish Lights, that the letter of the Harbour Commissioners, as requested by you, has been submitted for the consideration of the Board of Trade. They desire me to observe that either the rock is dangerous to the shipping of Cork, or it is not; if it is, that trade ought to pay for the removal in proportion to the benefit to be conferred on them; if it is not, the Harbour Commissioners should cease from asking for the requisite funds from other sources.

The Secretary,
Commissioners of Irish Lights.

I am, &c.
(signed)   C. Cecil Trevor.

— No. 26. —

Board of Trade to War Office.

(H. 2328.)

Board of Trade, Harbour Department,
Whitehall, 1 July 1868.

Sir,

I am directed by the Board of Trade to acknowledge the receipt of your letter of the 10th ult., enclosing copy of a Report by the Director of the Royal Engineer Establishment at Chatham, suggesting a survey of Daunt's Rock, and requesting that Sir J. Pakington may be informed whether the Board of Trade will furnish the requisite funds.

In reply I am to state, for the information of Sir J. Pakington, that as it is not determined who should pay for the work, if attempted, the Board of Trade regret that they are unable, under the present circumstances, to advance money to defray the expense of the survey proposed by the Director of the Royal Engineer Establishment.

The Under Secretary of State,
War Office.

I have, &c.
(signed)   C. Cecil Trevor.

— No. 27. —

Trinity House to Board of Trade.

(H. 1746.)

Trinity House, London,
10 April 1872.

Sir,

I am directed to transmit, for the information of the Board of Trade, the accompanying correspondence which has passed between the Irish Commissioners and this Corporation, upon the subject of placing a fog horn at Roche's Point, county Cork, in lieu of the bell thereat, from which it will be seen that the Elder Brethren have accorded their statutory approval to the alteration as proposed.

The Assistant Secretary,
Harbour Department, Board of Trade.

I am, &c.
(signed)   Robin Allen.

Enclosures in No. 27.

Irish Lights Office, Dublin,
27 February 1872.

Sir,

I am directed to forward herewith copy of a letter from the Cork Harbour Commissioners, under date 26th ultimo, with copy of a letter transmitted by them from the Harbour Master at Queenstown, as to the necessity for a more efficient fog signal at Roche's Point, near entrance of Cork Harbour; also copy of a letter from Mr. Roche, of London, offering to erect a steam fog signal, at an expense of 760 l., provided one-third of same is borne by the Cork Harbour Board, who, however, consider such an application of their funds would not come properly within their province.

The Board having referred those documents to the Committee of Inspection for report, I am to forward copy of same for the consideration of the Elder Brethren, and which report has been approved by the Commissioners of Irish Lights, who consider that if Mr. Roche contributes two-thirds of the expense for a Daboll's fog signal, the remaining portion may fairly be charged upon the Mercantile Marine Fund; I am, therefore, to request you will move the Elder Brethren to give their statutory sanction to the placing of a fog signal, of the above description, at Roche's Point.

The Secretary, Trinity House, London.

I am, &c.
(signed)   W. Lees.

Harbour Commissioners' Office, Cork,
26 January 1872.

Sir,

I am directed by the Board of Cork Harbour Commissioners to transmit, for the consideration of the Commissioners of Irish Lights, copy of a report made by the Harbour Master at Queenstown, recommending the erection of a fog signal at Roche's Point, near the entrance to Cork Harbour.

I also enclose copy of a letter received from Mr. Hugh H. Roche, London, proposing to erect a steam fog signal, at an expense of 760 l., provided one-third of the expense was borne by this Board.

The Commissioners desire me to express, as their unanimous opinion, that the establishment of such a form of fog signal would be of the greatest importance to vessels using the Port of Cork, but consider that such an application of their funds would not come properly within their province, but consider it advisable to bring the subject under the notice of the authority properly constituted to entertain such a subject.

The Secretary
To the Commissioners of Irish Lights, Dublin.

I am, &c.
(signed)   William Donegan,
Secretary.

Fog Signal, Roche's Point, Cork Harbour.

Having carefully considered the above subject, it is my decided opinion that this now most important port of call should have some efficient fog signal at Roche's Point. I know of one valuable steamer having been lost, and another put on shore, besides several sailing vessels, for want of an efficient signal in fog.

The bell at present should be   , and placed on the top of the cliff, instead of, as it is, under it; as it is, every mariner using the port condemns it as useless.

I think from what I have learned from the commanders of the steamers trading to America, who are not supposed to stop for fog, that there is a screeching whistle on Cape Race quite different from the ordinary whistle used on board steamers, and thus not to be mistaken for one of them; this would be the proper fog signal for Roche's Point, in connection with the fog bell, if placed so above recommended.

Failing the above, a heavy piece of ordnance fired at intervals, differing from the practice at present on board ship, with proper notice thereof, say, for example, one minute between each explosion, three to take place at a time, with an interval of three minutes, this may answer; at all events something should be done at once, and thus keep up the high character of your magnificent harbour.

Allow me to add, the leading light upon the eastern bank is much required, as requested by the commanders of the Cork Steam Ship Company.

(signed)   *H. H. O'Bryen.*

Fog Signals.

100, Palmerston Buildings, Old Broad-street,
London, 22 January 1871.

Dear Sir,

I notice this subject has been under discussion at your Board. I beg now to renew my offer of July last, viz., to erect one of these signals at or near Cork Harbour, the place to be selected by your Board; the cost will be 760 *l.*; and if your Board will subscribe one-third of the amount, I will use every endeavour to raise the balance by subscriptions from the Marine Insurance Companies, shipowners, &c., of England. I have already made great advances in this direction, but they do not feel called upon to subscribe the whole amount themselves.

I am, &c.
(signed)   *H. H. Roche.*

W. Dorman, Esq., Secretary,
Cork Harbour Board.

Copy of Report by Committee of Inspection on Letter from Cork Harbour Board, calling Attention to the necessity of placing a more efficient Fog Signal at Roche's Point.

The Committee recommend that application be made to the Trinity Board to be allowed to place a Daboll's Fog Signal at Roche's Point, and that Mr. Roche's offer, with reference to its erection, assuming it to be the same, be forwarded to them.

Irish Lights Office, Dublin, 6 February 1872.

Extract from Letter to Irish Commissioners, dated 14th March 1872.

"As regards the proposal for a better fog signal at Roche's Point, the Elder Brethren are ready, if the expense of its erection and maintenance, as adverted to in your letter of the 27th ultimo, can be satisfactorily settled, to accord their sanitary sanction to that which will undoubtedly be a more efficient signal."

Irish Lights Office, Dublin,
6 April 1872.

Sir,

With reference to the concluding paragraph of your letter of 14th ultimo, in reply to my letter of 27th February last, the Elder Brethren stating that they are ready to give their statutory sanction for the placing of a better fog signal at Roche's Point, at entrance of Cork Harbour, if the expense of its erection and maintenance, as adverted to, can be satisfactorily settled, I am now to forward, for any observations the Elder Brethren may be pleased to offer, copy of a letter from Mr. Roche, under date 6th instant, in reply to a letter addressed to him by this Board on the 29th ult., a copy of which herewith.

A copy of Mr. Roche's original letter has been transmitted in mine of 27th February.

I am, &c.
(signed)   *W. Lees.*

Secretary, Trinity House, London.

Sir,
Irish Lights Office, Dublin,
30 March 1872.

THE Cork Harbour Commissioners having forwarded to this Board copy of a letter forwarded to them, under date 22nd January last, in which you state you renew your offer to erect an improved fog signal at or near Cork Harbour, the place to be selected by them, at a cost of 760 L., provided the Harbour Board will subscribe one-third of this amount, you using your endeavour to raise the balance, I am directed by the Commissioners of Irish Lights, whose sanction is necessary, to request you will be so good as to furnish them with a full description of the fog signal, together with a plan or drawing of same, also the name of the maker, and that you will be good enough to afford them every information in your power.

H. H. Roche, Esq.

I am, &c.
(signed) W. Lees.

Sir,
London, 6 April 1872.

YOUR favour 30th March to hand. In reply, beg to say that as soon as I have the consent of your Board I shall endeavour to carry out the proposal I made to the Cork Harbour Board, and to set for them a fac-simile fog signal to that erected for the Canadian Government, my plans and specifications for which are endorsed by them, although at the moment I am not free to send you them, this being a new invention.

None of these signals having as yet been made here, I am not able to give you names of makers, but I have made arrangements with a highly respectable firm to construct this necessary works.

Be good enough to inform your Board that I hold myself at liberty, if the proposition be accepted, to make use of their approval in statements of such facts to the underwriters.

W. Lees, Esq., Secretary,
Irish Lights Office.

I have, &c.
(signed) H. H. Roche.

Sir,
Trinity House, London, 10 April 1872.

I AM directed to acknowledge receipt of your letter, dated 9th instant, enclosing copy of one from Mr. Roche, further as to the proposed fog signal at Roche's Point, and in reply thereto I am to observe, that Mr. Roche's letter does not enable the Elder Brethren to judge whether the signal proposed is the best which could be placed, but that having regard to the terms on which it is intended to be provided, and to its being doubtless an improvement in the existing arrangement, the Elder Brethren have no objection to offer, so long as the Irish Commissioners are satisfied that it is expedient to proceed further in the matter.

W. Lees, Esq., Dublin.

I am, &c.
(signed) Robin Allen.

— No. 22. —

Board of Trade to Commissioners of Irish Lights.

(H. 1746.)

Board of Trade, Harbour Department,
Whitehall Gardens, 16 April 1872.

Sir,

REFERRING to the correspondence which has taken place between the Corporation of Trinity House and the Commissioners of Irish Lights, relative to the placing of a fog horn at Roche's Point, county Cork, and which has been referred to this Department, I am directed by the Board of Trade to observe, for the information of the Commissioners, that it does not appear in the correspondence in question whether the maintenance of the fog horn is provided for, and I am to inquire whether, when it is erected, it is to be handed over to the Commissioners, or what arrangement is to be made.

I am also to ask whether the signal is to be placed on the lighthouse property at Roche's Point.

The Secretary,
Commissioners of Irish Lights.

I am, &c.
(signed) C. Cecil Trevor.

— No. 29. —

Trinity House to Board of Trade.

(H. 3190.)

Trinity House, London,
5 July 1872.

Sir,

ADVERTING to my letter of the 10th April last, enclosing, for the information of the Board of Trade, correspondence which had passed between the Commissioners of Irish Lights and this Board upon the subject of placing an improved fog signal on Roche's Point, entrance to Cork Harbour, and stating that the Elder Brethren had approved the proposed alteration, I am now to forward further correspondence upon the subject, and to state that the Elder Brethren, agreeing in opinion with the Irish Commissioners that no further delay should take place pending any arrangement which might be arrived at with Mr. Roche, have accorded their statutory sanction to the erection of a fog signal thereat, of the most improved description.

I am to request that the enclosures, with my letter of the 10th April, together with those of this day, being in original, may be returned.

I am, &c.

The Assistant Secretary,
Harbour Department, Board of Trade.

(signed)   Robin Allen.

Enclosures in No. 29.

Irish Lights Office, Dublin,
27 June 1872.

Sir,

WITH reference to your letter of 24th April last, relative to Mr. Roche's suggestion as to proposed fog signal on Roche's Point, I am directed to forward copy of a letter from that gentleman, under date 17th inst., stating he has instructed Mr. Crowe, O.E., to put himself in communication with the Trinity House on the subject, the Commissioners of Irish Lights direct me to say they will be glad to be informed of the result of such communication.

I am to add a further letter has been received urging the necessity of providing an efficient system of fog signal at Roche's Point, from Cork Harbour Board.

I am, &c.

The Secretary, Trinity House, London.

(signed)   W. Lees.

100, Palmerston Buildings, Old Broad-street,
London, 17 June 1872.

Sir,

IN accordance with the request of your favour, I handed these papers to Mr. Crowe, O.E., of 9, New Broad-street, with instructions for him to put himself in communication with the Trinity Board here, and give them all particulars, and as soon as anything transpires we will at once communicate with you.

I have, &c.

The Secretary, Irish Lights Office.

(signed)   H. H. Roche.

Irish Lights Office, Dublin,
1 July 1872.

Sir,

IN reference to the correspondence which has taken place, and to your letter of the 10th April last, in connection with the proposition of Mr. Roche as to an improved fog signal on Roche's Point, I am directed to forward copy of a further letter from the Cork Harbour Board, urging the necessity for an efficient fog signal being placed, and calling attention to the stranding of the steam ship "Nevada." The Commissioners having had before them Mr. Roche's letter of the 17th ultimo, a copy of which was sent you on the 27th ultimo, consider the matter of so much importance that no further delay should take place, and which doubtless must occur pending any final arrangement being arrived at in connection with Mr. Roche's suggestion, and they direct me to express their opinion that a fog trumpet of the most improved description be at once procured for the above object, and I am to request the statutory sanction of the Elder Brethren accordingly, and also that they will be so good as to inform this Board the description of fog trumpet which they, from experience, consider the most efficient and suitable.

I am, &c.

The Secretary, Trinity House, London.

(signed)   W. Lees.

Sir,   Cork, 21 June 1872.

With reference to my communication dated 24th January last, enclosing a report of the harbour master at Queenstown, and expressing the views of this Board upon the necessity of providing an efficient system of fog signal at the entrance of Cork Harbour, I am directed by the Board of Harbour Commissioners to request that you will be so good as to move your Board to take prompt action in the matter, which is there (the Commissioners) judgment is of such grave import to the mercantile marine of the country. You are doubtless aware of the importance of Cork Harbour as a port of call for mailing and steam ships trading from all parts of the world, which, in the opinion of the Commissioners, is a strong ground for urging this matter on the attention of the Commissioners of Irish Lights, and of early precaution being taken to protect the shipping making for Cork Harbour.

I am furthermore to direct the attention of the Commissioners of Irish Lights to the stranding of the steam ship "Nevada," and to the near escape from total loss of that vessel outside Cork Harbour on Monday the 16th inst., an occurrence which, in the opinion of the Board, would have been avoided, did any proper means of signalling during the fog exist to warn the vessel of her proximity to land.

                              I am, &c.
                     (signed)   W. Denegan.

The Secretary, Irish Lights Office.

───────

                        Trinity House, London, E.C.,
                                  3 July 1872.
Sir,
Adverting to previous correspondence upon the subject of an improved fog signal to be placed on Roche's Point, I am directed to acquaint you, for the information of the Irish Commissioners, that the Elder Brethren fully recognise the advisability of such an improvement, and I am accordingly to convey to you the statutory sanction of this Corporation to its erection.

I am to add, with reference to the latter part of your letter of the 1st inst., relative to the description of fog signal which the Elder Brethren would suggest should be adopted, that they have referred the matter to Mr. Douglass for his opinion, and that they will communicate again with the Irish Commissioners on receipt of his report.

                              I am, &c.
                     (signed)   Robin Allen.

The Secretary,
Irish Lights Office, Dublin.

───────

— No. 30. —

Board of Trade to Trinity House.

(H. 3190.)

                  Board of Trade, Harbour Department,
                      Whitehall Gardens, 22 July 1872.
Sir,
I am directed by the Board of Trade to acknowledge the receipt of your letter of the 5th instant, forwarding farther correspondence between the Elder Brethren and the Commissioners of Irish Lights, on the subject of placing a fog signal on Roche's Point, county Cork.

In reply, I am to state, for the information of the Elder Brethren of the Trinity House, that the Board of Trade, as at present advised, are not disposed to question the propriety of the establishment of efficient fog signals at Cork Harbour and its approaches; but they think it is a question for consideration whether Roche's Point, at the entrance of Cork Harbour, is the best site for a first-class fog signal. Looking to the configuration of the coast and the recessed position of Roche's Point, it might seem desirable that the most powerful signals should be placed in advance of the harbour, say at Roberts' Head, on the south-west, if there be no insuperable difficulty, and at Poor Head on the south-east. Off the former lies Daunt Rock, at a distance of four and a half miles from Roche's Point, too far to permit the steam whistle to give warning during south-westerly gales and thick mist, whilst Roberts' Head would cut off the sound of the Roche's Point signal from reaching the recessed bay between

0.57.   D 4

between the former and Kinsale Head, should a ship get there inadvertently at times when the signal might otherwise have been heard.

On the other hand Poor Head, which is three miles to the east of Roche's Point, would intercept the sound for two and a half miles seaward of Smith's Rock, near Ballycotton Island Lighthouse, and the signal consequently might not be so advantageously placed as a warning to the ships approaching from the eastward, as it would be on Poor Head, which commands a clear range on either side.

It might therefore be urged that a ship making for Cork Harbour, either from east or west, should first receive timely warning from these advanced posts, and guided by the signals thereat, could hit the entrance pretty close until she heard the bell or some other sound instrument at Roche's Point.

I have therefore to request that you will move the Elder Brethren of the Trinity House to be so good as to favour this Board with any observations they may desire to make on the views expressed above as to the situation of the proposed fog signal, and I am to state that the Board have invited the observations of the Liverpool Shipowners' Association, and the Liverpool Steam Shipowners' Association, on this subject, which is naturally of great importance to them.

The enclosures contained in your letter, together with those in your letter of the 10th April, are herewith returned as requested.

I am, &c.

(signed)   C. Cecil Trevor.

The Secretary, Trinity House.

— No. 81. —

Board of Trade to Commissioners of Irish Lights.

(H. 3190.)

Board of Trade, Harbour Department,
Sir,   Whitehall Gardens, 23 July 1872.

REFERRING to further correspondence between the Elder Brethren of the Trinity House and the Commissioners of Irish Lights on the subject of placing a fog signal at Roche's Point, which has been forwarded to this department, I am directed by the Board of Trade to state, for the information of the Commissioners of Irish Lights, that the Board of Trade, as at present advised, are not disposed to question the propriety of the establishment of efficient fog signals at Cork Harbour and its approaches; but they think it is a question for consideration whether Roche's Point, at the entrance of Cork Harbour, is the best site for a first-class fog signal. Looking to the configuration of the coast and the recessed position of Roche's Point, it might seem desirable that the most powerful signals should be placed in advance of the harbour, say at Roberts' Head, on the south-west, if there be no insuperable difficulty, and at Poor Head on the south-east. Off the former lies Daunt Rock, at a distance of four-and-a-half miles from Roche's Point, too far to permit the steam whistle to give warning during south-westerly gales and thick mist, while Roberts' Head would cut off the sound of the Roche's Point signal from reaching the recessed bay between the former and Kinsale Head, should a ship get there inadvertently, at times when the signal might otherwise have been heard.

On the other hand Poor Head, which is three miles to the east of Roche's Point, would intercept the sound for two-and-a-half miles seaward of Smith's Rock, near Ballycotton Island Lighthouse, and the signal consequently might not be so advantageously placed as a warning to the ships approaching from the eastward, as it would be on Poor Head, which commands a clear range on either side.

It might therefore be urged that a ship making for Cork Harbour, either from east or west, should first receive timely warning from these advanced posts, and guided by the signals thereat, could hit the entrance pretty close until she heard the bell or some other sound instrument at Roche's Point.

I am

I am therefore to request that you will move the Commissioners of Irish Lights to be so good as to favour this Board with any observations they may desire to offer on the views expressed above as to the situation of the proposed fog signal, and I am to state that the Board have invited the observations of the Liverpool Shipowners' Association and the Liverpool Steam Shipowners' Association upon this subject, which is naturally of great importance to them.

In conclusion, I am also to request that you will call the attention of the Commissioners to the letter from this Board of the 16th April last (H. 1746) on the same subject, to which no reply has as yet been received.

I am, &c.,
(signed) C. Cecil Trevor.

The Secretary, Commissioners of Irish Lights.

— No. 22. —

Board of Trade to Liverpool Shipowners' Association.

(H. 3190.)

Board of Trade, Harbour Department,
Whitehall Gardens, 23 July 1872.

Sir,

I am directed by the Board of Trade to state that a correspondence has lately taken place between the Commissioners of Irish Lights and the Elder Brethren of the Trinity House on the subject of a proposal to place an improved fog signal on Roche's Point, County Cork. Both these bodies are agreed as to the desirability of doing so, and the Board desire me to state to you for the information of the Shipowners' Association their views on the proposal of the Commissioners of Irish Lights and Elder Brethren.

The Board of Trade, as at present advised, are not disposed to question the propriety of the establishment of efficient fog signals at Cork Harbour and its approaches, but they think it is a question for consideration whether Roche's Point at the entrance of Cork Harbour is the best site for a first-class fog signal. Looking to the configuration of the coast and the recessed position of Roche's Point, it might seem desirable that the most powerful signals should be placed in advance of the harbour, say at Roberts' Head on the south-west, if there be no insuperable difficulty, and at Poor Head on the south-east. Of the former lies Daunt Rock, at a distance of four-and-a-half miles from Roche's Point, too far to permit the steam whistle to give warning during south-westerly gales and thick mist, while Roberts' Head would cut off the sound of the Roches' Point signal from reaching the recessed bay between the former and Kinsale Head, should a ship get there inadvertently, at times when the signal might otherwise have been heard.

On the other hand Poor Head, which is three miles to the south-east of Roche's Point, would intercept the sound for two-and-a-half miles seaward of Smith's Rock, near Ballycotton Island Lighthouse; and the signal consequently might not be so advantageously placed as a warning to the ships approaching from the eastward, as it would be on Poor Head, which commands a clear range on either side.

It might therefore be urged that it would be better that a ship making for Cork Harbour, either from the east or west, should first receive timely warning from these advanced posts, and guided by signals thereon could hit the entrance pretty close, until she heard the bell or other sounding instrument at Roche's Point.

I am therefore to request that you will move the Association to be so good as to favour this Board with any observations they may desire to make on the views expressed above as to the situation of the proposed fog signal.

I am, &c.,
(signed) Cecil C. Trevor.

The Secretary, Shipowners' Association, Liverpool.

— No. 33. —

Board of Trade to Liverpool Steam Shipowners' Association.

(H. 3190.)

(Similar Letter to No. 32.)

— No. 34. —

Liverpool Shipowners' Association to Board of Trade.

(H. 3534.)

Sir,   Liverpool, 31 July 1872.
We are directed by the Committee for managing the affairs of this Association to acknowledge the receipt of your letter of the 23rd instant, which has
been submitted to them at a meeting held this afternoon.
We send you copy of resolution come to on this subject.

We are, &c.
(signed)   Field & Moss,
Secretaries.

The Assistant Secretary,
Harbour Department, Board of Trade,
Whitehall Gardens, London, S.W.

Enclosure in No. 34.

At a Meeting of the Committee of the Liverpool Shipowners' Association, held on
Wednesday the 31st July 1872.

Present :—Philip Nelson, Esq. (in the chair), &c., &c., &c.

Approaches to Cork Harbour.—Proposed Fog Signal.

It was resolved—That in the opinion of the Association it would be very advisable
that efficient fog signals should be placed on the promontories both to the eastward and
westward of the approach to Cork Harbour, viz., the old Head of Kinsale to the westward, and Poor Head to the eastward, and this Association further suggest that Daunt's
Rock should have a light-ship with a fog bell placed over it, which they think could well
be made into a pilot and (if practicable) a telegraph and postal station.

Extracted from the proceedings.

Field & Moss, Secretaries.

— No. 35. —

The Liverpool Steam Shipowners' Association to Board of Trade.

(H. 3787.)

Sir,   Liverpool, 19 August 1872.
Your letter, H. 3190, upon the subject of proposed fog signals near Queenstown, has been carefully considered by the General Committee of this Association, and several of the masters of large steamers engaged in the trade between
Liverpool and New York have been consulted upon the question, and I now beg
to lay before you the views which the Association adopt.
They agree with the Board of Trade in considering that it is advisable that
there

there should be fog signals on both sides of Queenstown Harbour, instead of one signal at Roche's Point alone, and that the signal to the south-east should be at Poor Head.

With regard to the position of the signal to the south-west, they are of opinion that it will be much more serviceable at the Old Head of Kinsale than anywhere else. On that point being made, and the bearings taken with a cast of the lead at the same time, a fair approximate position for shaping a course towards Queenstown will be obtained. It will be advisable to provide that the two signals should be different altogether in character, so that it will be impossible to mistake the one for the other; for notwithstanding the distance which will intervene between them, mistakes might arise in very thick weather. It is very important to have a signal upon Roche's Point, and the Association would suggest that a very powerful bell should be placed there in lieu of the small and wholly inefficient bell now used. With regard to Daunt's Rock, the Association trust that there has been no change in the opinion of the Commissioners of Irish Lights stated in their letter of the 5th April last to this Association, that it will be proper to erect a lighthouse on Roberts' Head, giving a white light of a distinctive character, and showing a beam of red light over the rock.

Until some means be taken efficiently to mark Daunt's Rock, the principal point of danger upon the coast near Queenstown will still remain unguarded.

I am, &c.

(signed)   *Greg Hill,*
              Secretary.

The Assistant Secretary,
Harbour Department, Board of Trade.

— No. 86. —

Trinity House to Board of Trade.

(H. 3788.)   Trinity House, London, E.C.,
Sir,   19 August 1872.

HAVING laid before the Board your letter of the 23rd ult., further on the subject of placing a fog signal on Roche's Point, at the entrance to Cork Harbour, and submitting for consideration whether it may be desirable that in addition thereto powerful signals should also be placed in advance of the harbour, say at Roberts' Head or Poor Head; I am directed to acquaint you that the Elder Brethren having again given careful consideration to the whole subject, are of opinion that the question of establishing three signals for this one harbour would be very much one of expense, and no doubt with the valuable property daily resorting to Cork Harbour, such an outlay might be justifiable; but it must be for those upon whom that expense would fall to say whether they are prepared and willing to bear it.

If it is understood that a fog trumpet can be established on Roche's Point with an expenditure of only one-third of its cost price, out of the Mercantile Marine Fund, it might, in conjunction with the Bell Buoy which marks the Daunt Rock, be made, in the opinion of the Elder Brethren, sufficient for entering the harbour; but if it be thought worth while to establish the additional signals on Poor Head and Roberts' Head, care must be taken to secure in the first place a sufficiently distinct character for each.

It seems to the Elder Brethren that in that case a powerful fog whistle would be more suitable for Poor Head than for Roche's Point (assuming that there are facilities for supplying water, fuel, and necessaries for the keepers), and would no doubt be a great boon to vessels approaching the harbour from the eastward.

Upon Roberts' Head the Elder Brethren are of opinion that a gun would be the most effective to give sufficient warning that vessels were approaching the vicinity of Daunt's Rock, and would lead them to look out for the Bell Boat, which the Elder Brethren have themselves found very effective in thick fog.

If these outlying signals are placed, there will be less necessity for an expensive signal on Roche's Point, as already proposed, and the question of its size might be reconsidered.

                                                 The

The annual expenditure in respect of these three signals is a matter requiring serious consideration. but if the local trade, or those interested in vessels calling at this harbour, are willing to contribute the necessary tolls for their maintenance, the Elder Brethren are prepared to give their statutory sanction to the suggested establishments ; but they, before doing so, would be glad to hear the opinion which the Board of Trade may obtain from Liverpool on the subject, in answer to their invitation.

I am, &c.
(signed)   J. Inglis,

The Assistant Secretary,
Harbour Department, Board of Trade.

— No. 37. —

Commissioners of Irish Lights to Board of Trade.

(H. 3821.)   Irish Lights Office, Westmoreland-street,
Sir,   Dublin, 22 August 1872.

I am directed by the Commissioners of Irish Lights to acknowledge the receipt of your letter of the 23rd ultimo (H. 3190) on subject of improved fog signals being placed at the approaches to Cork Harbour, and I have in reply to state, that this Board fully concur with the suggestion contained in your letter of placing a powerful fog signal on Roberts' Head and also on Poor Head, as there can be no doubt such signals would be of great advantage to vessels approaching that harbour in thick weather. The Board, however, consider these signals should possess perfectly distinctive characteristics, and would also suggest that the very inferior fog signal at Roche's Point be largely improved. I am to state, that the Inspector of Lights concur in the above.

With reference to the observation contained in the concluding paragraph of your letter, stating "the Board of Trade had not received any reply to their letter " of the 17th April last (H. 1746) on the same subject," I am to acquaint you, the Commissioners not having heard anything satisfactory of or from Mr. Hoche, are not in a position to make any reply, and are inclined to consider his proposition as at an end.

I am, &c.
(signed)   W. Lees.

The Assistant Secretary,
Harbour Department, Board of Trade.

— No. 38. —

Board of Trade to Commissioners of Irish Lights.

(H. 3821.)   Board of Trade, Harbour Department,
Sir,   Whitehall Gardens, 3 September 1872.

With reference to your letter of the 22nd ultimo, relating to placing fog signals at the entrance to Cork Harbour, I am directed by the Board of Trade to transmit to you, for the information of the Commissioners of Irish Lights, copies of letters which have been received from the Liverpool Shipowners' Association and the Liverpool Steam Shipowners' Association on the subject.

In order to assist them in forming an opinion upon the several proposals which have been made, the Board of Trade would be glad to be furnished with separate estimates of the expense of the carrying out and maintenance of each portion of these proposals, as well as of the proposal which was contained in the letter from this office of the 23rd July last (H. 3190).

I am, &c.
(signed)   C. Cecil Trevor.

The Secretary, Commissioners of Irish Lights.

— No. 39. —

Board of Trade to Trinity House.

(H. 3821.) Board of Trade, Harbour Department,
Sir, Whitehall Gardens, 9 September 1872.

WITH reference to your letter of the 30th ultimo, relative to the best mode of marking the entrance of Cork Harbour, and the wish which is expressed in the concluding paragraph of that letter, that the Elder Brethren may hear the opinion which the Board of Trade may obtain from Liverpool on the subject, I am directed by the Board of Trade to transmit to you, for the information of the Corporation of Trinity House, copies of letters which have been received from the Liverpool Shipowners' Association, and the Liverpool Steam Shipowners' Association, on the subject, and to state that the Board will be glad to be favoured with any further observations that the Elder Brethren may desire to offer.

The Secretary, Trinity House.

I am, &c.
(signed) C. Cecil Trevor.

— No. 40. —

Commissioners of Irish Lights to Board of Trade.

(H. 4224.) Irish Lights Office, Westmoreland-street,
Sir, Dublin, 2 October 1872.

I AM directed by the Commissioners of Irish Lights to acknowledge the receipt of your letter of the 3rd ultimo (H. 3821), enclosing copies of the letters received from the Liverpool Shipowners' Association and the Liverpool Steam Shipowners' Association, on the subject of fog signals off and at the entrance of Cork Harbour, and requesting the opinion of this Board on the several proposals, and also asking for separate estimates of the probable cost of each, as well as those suggested in your letter of the 23rd July last (H. 3190).

In reply, I have now to enclose copy of a report from the engineer of this Board, furnishing approximate estimates on these various matters, from which it appears—

		£.	s.	d.
1st.	Cost of a powerful Fog Bell at Roche's Point -	770	—	—
2nd.	A second order Light on Roberts' Head -	8,100	—	—
	Annual Cost of Maintenance -	290	—	—
3rd.	A third order Light on Roberts' Head -	2,340	—	—
	Annual Cost of Maintenance -	175	—	—
4th.	A Light-ship off Daunt's Rock -	6,800	—	—
	Annual Cost of Maintenance -	1,800	—	—
5th.	A Fog Horn Establishment at Poer Head -	1,600	—	—
	Annual Cost of Maintenance -	80	—	—
6th.	A Gun at Old Head of Kinsale, say -	800	—	—
	Annual Cost of Maintenance, exclusive of Powder	84	10	—

Having carefully considered these various suggestions, this Board is of the opinion that, considering the enormous amount of shipping calling at or off

0.67. B 3 Queenstown

Queenstown (little short of 3,000,000 tons per annum), the marking of its approaches ought to be made as perfectly efficient as modern science can devise. We therefore recommend that, instead of the existing almost worthless bell at Roche's Point, there should be substituted the large one suggested by Mr. Sloane.

As respects the Poor Head, this Board fully concurs in the view, that a powerful fog trumpet (or possibly a gun) should be placed on it, as doubtless it would often be of great value in enabling a ship to ascertain her exact position.

As regards the better marking of Daunt's Rock, this Board cannot perceive any grounds for altering the views expressed in their letter of the 6th March last, and for the reasons therein given, rejects the idea of placing a light-ship off that rock, and continues of the opinion that for its most effective marking, a light ought to be placed on Roberts' Head, with or without a fog signal. If the latter proposal be adopted, and a permanent establishment be maintained there, this Board is of the opinion that the moderate additional cost of a lighthouse on that head would be fully justified. It is gratifying to this Board to find that the Liverpool Steam Shipowners' Association fully concur in these views.

In reference to the suggestion of that association, that a fog signal should be placed on the Old Head of Kinsale, as the best point for such, to the west-ward of Queenstown, this Board is of the opinion that if such an idea be adopted, it may be unnecessary to place one on Roberts' Head, placing there a light only, and that if such signal be placed on the Old Head, it should be gun; but this Board is not without grave doubts as to its expediency, or that it could be made an effective fog signal. The platform on which the lighthouse establish-ment is placed is from 130 to 140 feet above the sea, and as sound has a tendency to pass upward rather than downwards or horizontal, it is questionable if a gun placed at such a height would be heard at any considerable distance, and therefore it might rather lead into danger than out of it. The gun could not, with any safety, be placed lower down the headland, because in bad weather the sea washes it to its top. The Commissioners, however, have no hesitation in recommending, that this important headland be fit with gun, and that possess the facility of increasing the power of the light according to the state of the weather.

There is one point which has not yet been adverted to in the various con-siderations in relation to the improving the marking of the approaches to Queens-town, which this Board is desirous of bringing before the consideration of the Board of Trade, viz., the very inferior character of the light at Roche's Point. Were it only a light to guide ships into Queenstown and Cork, it might be deemed sufficient as a harbour light for such a purpose, but considering the vast amount of shipping resorting to that part of the coast from all parts of the world, it is in reality one of the most important lights on the coast. This Board is of the opinion, that under these circumstances, and lying as it does so much resorted, it ought to be made as effective a light as possible. Instead, therefore, of its being a second order catoptric light showing red to seaward, this Board considers that it ought to be a first order dioptric of gas, of a distinctive character, showing *white*. Were this change adopted, together with the foregoing sugges-tions, this Board believes that the approaches to Queenstown would be marked as effectively as can be desired.

I am, &c.

The Assistant Secretary,   (signed)   Owen Armstrong,
Harbour Department, Board of Trade.   for Secretary.

Enclosure in No. 40.

Sir,   Irish Lights Office, 12 September 1872.
As directed, I have read letters from Board of Trade relative to placing fog signals at the entrance to Cork Harbour, also copies of letters enclosed from Liverpool Shipowners' Association, and also from Liverpool Steam Shipowners' Association, along with copy of

letter of 22rd July last (H. 8190), and in compliance with Board's order of 6th instant, I have prepared approximate estimates of the different proposals as follows:—

	£	s.	d.
Large Fog Bell at Roche's Point, say 80 cwt., at 1 s. 6 d. per lb.	420	—	—
Machine for ditto	200	—	—
Erection and Carriage	150	—	—
	£ 770	**—**	**—**
Light on Roberts' Head, if second order:			
Buildings	1,800	—	—
Lantern	800	—	—
Apparatus	600	—	—
	£ 3,100	**—**	**—**
Light on Roberts' Head, if third order:			
Buildings	1,800	—	—
Lantern	460	—	—
Apparatus	850	—	—
	£ 3,240	**—**	**—**
Maintenance of second order, per annum	220	—	—
Maintenance of third order, per annum	175	—	—
Light-ship off Daunt's Rock :			
Cost of Ship	8,800	—	—
Maintenance, per annum	1,800	—	—
Fog House on Poor Head	680	—	—
Dwelling for Keeper	700	—	—
Maintenance	80	—	—
Erection and Carriage	350	—	—
	£ 1,680	**—**	**—**
Gun, probably for Old Head, similar to that at Bailtlis Island :			
Dwelling for Gunner, with Magazine and Carriage	800	—	—
Pay to Gunner	34	10	—

I am not able either to arrive at size of gun or price. I have endeavoured to estimate the probable cost of each of the fog signals, but their positions is a matter for the Board's consideration; and although a fog gun is not suggested in the correspondence, I have presumed that as it is considered advisable that the marking of Poor Head and Old Head should be different, a gun would be probably adopted at either place.

I am, &c.

W. Lees, Esq., &c. &c.

(signed)   John S. Sloane,

— No. 41. —

Trinity House to Board of Trade.

(H. 4243.)

Sir,

Trinity House, London,
3 October 1872.

Having laid before the Board your letter (H. 8768) of the 3rd instant, enclosing copies of a correspondence received from the Liverpool Shipowners' Association and the Liverpool Steam Shipowners' Association, relative to the best mode of marking the entrance to Cork Harbour. I am directed to submit the following observations for the information of the Board of Trade.

The suggestions of the two associations coincide with that of the Elder Brethren as to placing a fog signal on Poor Head and one at Roche's Point, but both concur in recommending the Old Head of Kinsale as the site for the

Western signal, proposing also to mark Daunt's Rock, the one by a light vessel, the other by a lighthouse on Robert's Head.

As respects Daunt's Rock and Robert's Head, the Elder Brethren have more than once expressed their opinion that a light on Roberts' Head could only be useful as a thwart light for marking Daunt's Rock, and that the best way of warning navigation of that danger would be to place a light-ship to the southward of it; they still remain of this opinion, and would add that a powerful fog signal should be placed on board the light-ship. The Old Head of Kinsale, being 16 miles from Hocko's Point, is at too great a distance for use as a signal station for vessels entering Cork Harbour.

The Commissioners of Irish Lights have expressed an opinion that there is not good holding ground for a light-vessel in the proposed position, but the Elder Brethren are not aware that this opinion has been confirmed by actual survey.

Hitherto the establishment of a light vessel to mark the Daunt's Rock has been a subject of question as respects the authority upon whom the expense of it should fall. The Elder Brethren have concurred with the Board of Trade in thinking that the cost should not be borne by the passing trade, but by the local authorities, while the harbour authorities of Cork have considered that the charges should not be borne solely by the trade of the port. If, however, it may be assumed that the Liverpool shipowners and marine shipowners' societies, in recommending the establishment of lights and signals, imply their willingness to pay for them, the Board of Trade may see fit to charge the cost and maintenance upon the Mercantile Marine Fund, and to levy a toll only upon vessels entering or calling for orders at Queenstown in the same manner as for the other local lights borne upon the Mercantile Marine Fund (see page III. of the Consolidated Tables of Light Duties), and the Elder Brethren would see no objection to such an arrangement.

It results, therefore, that if the financial arrangements can be satisfactorily settled, the Elder Brethren would be prepared to give their statutory sanction to place a light ship to the southward of Daunt's Rock, having on board a powerful fog signal, to establish a powerful fog signal on Poer Head, and another on Roche's Point, taking care that unmistakable distinction is maintained between the sounds of the different signals.

The nature and character of the various fog signals is a matter upon which the Elder Brethren desire to withhold their opinion until after the return of a committee of their body, who are at present investigating the subject in Canada and the United States of America.

I am, &c.
(signed)   Robin Allen.

The Assistant Secretary,
Harbour Department, Board of Trade.

— No. 42. —

Board of Trade to Trinity House.

(H. 4245.)   Board of Trade, Harbour Department,
Sir,   Whitehall Gardens, 11 October 1872.

WITH reference to previous correspondence on the subject of marking Cork Harbour, I am directed by the Board of Trade to transmit to you, for the information of the Corporation of Trinity House, the enclosed letter which has been received from the Commissioners of Irish Lights upon the subject, and to suggest that if possible the Corporation and the Commissioners should adopt a proposal which could be submitted by the Commissioners and sanctioned by the Corporation in the usual statutory manner, so that the Board of Trade could put it before the shipping interest, stating that on the understanding that the shipping which uses Cork Harbour, or calls off it, will pay a sufficient toll to defray such expenditure as may be incurred in improving the marking of the harbour, the Board

Board of Trade will sanction the expenditure which will be necessary to carry out the arrangement which may be finally agreed to.

The Secretary, Trinity House.

I am, &c.

(signed) *Thomas Gray.*

— No. 43. —

Board of Trade to Commissioners of Irish Lights.

(U. 4243.)

Board of Trade, Harbour Department, Whitehall Gardens, 11 October 1872.

Sir,

WITH reference to previous correspondence on the subject of marking Cork Harbour, I am directed by the Board of Trade to transmit to you, for the information of the Commissioners of Irish Lights, the enclosed letter which has been received from the Corporation of Trinity House upon the subject, and to suggest that, if possible, the Corporation and the Commissioners should adopt a proposal which could be submitted by the Commissioners and sanctioned by the Corporation in the usual statutory manner, so that the Board of Trade could put it before the shipping interest, stating that, on the understanding that the shipping which uses Cork Harbour, or calls off it, will pay a sufficient toll to defray such expenditure as may be incurred in improving the marking of the harbour, the Board of Trade will sanction the expenditure which will be necessary to carry out the arrangements which may be finally agreed to.

The Secretary,
Commissioners of Irish Lights.

I am, &c.

(signed) *Thomas Gray.*

— No. 44. —

Trinity House to Board of Trade.

(E. 5209.)

Trinity House, London, 6 December 1872.

Sir,

ADVERTING to previous correspondence, and more particularly to your letter dated 11th October last, on the subject of marking the approaches to Cork Harbour, I am directed to acquaint you, for the information of the Board of Trade, that with a view of expediting matters, the Elder Brethren suggested to the Irish Commissioners that a deputation from their Board should come to London, so that the subject might be fully discussed and some definite arrangement arrived at; and that this suggestion having been concurred in, a deputation consisting of Mr. Bewley, Mr. Crosthwait, Captain Knott, and Mr. Stirling, with Mr. Lees, the Secretary to the Board, met the Elder Brethren at this house on the 12th ultimo, and again on the 16th ultimo.

* * * *

I am now to enclose, for the information of the Board of Trade, the accompanying copies of correspondence consequent thereon, by which it will be seen that a definite proposal for the marking of Cork Harbour has received conditionally, on a satisfactory settlement of the financial question, the statutory sanction of this Corporation.

* * * *

The Assistant Secretary,
Harbour Department, Board of Trade.

I have, &c.

(signed) *Robin Allen.*

F

Enclosure 1, in No. 44

Sir,　　　　　　　　　　　　　Trinity House, London, 12 November 1872.

In conformity with the understanding come to at the conference between the deputation from the Commissioners for Irish Lights and the members of this Board, held yesterday at this house, on the subject of the best mode of lighting and otherwise marking the approaches to Cork Harbour, I am directed to transmit the following memorandum of the arrangements understood to be agreed on, and to state that on receiving from you a formal proposal in accordance therewith, the Elder Brethren will have great pleasure in giving their statutory sanction to the same.

First, then, having regard to the importance and constantly increasing amount of the trade using Cork Harbour, and to the desirability of offering every facility for navigation of a peculiarly rapid and valuable character, it was agreed, upon the understanding that an adequate toll be levied on vessels calling at Queenstown or Cork, for its due maintenance, that a light-ship be placed outside the Daunt's Rock, to show a red revolving light, and that it be also fitted with a powerful fog trumpet on the Holmes or Daboll principle, and worked by a Caloric engine.

2nd. That to assist the approach of vessels from the eastward a similar fog signal, but distinctive in the character of the blast, be placed on Poer Head, and a third or a large bell, at Roche's Point, and that the light at Roche's Point should be changed from red revolving to a 1st order dioptric (gas) white of distinctive character.

3rd. That having regard to these arrangements, the consideration of a fog signal at the Old Head of Kinsale is deferred, particularly as the question of a fog signal of this character at the Fastnet, where it will best mark the landfall of the Irish coast, will shortly come under consideration, but that if the Irish Commissioners are desirous of improving the light at Kinsale by the substitution of gas for oil, the Elder Brethren have no objection to offer.

I am, &c.

The Secretary,　　　　　　　　　　(signed)　　R. Allen.
Irish Lights Commissioners.

Enclosure 2, in No. 44.

Sir,　　　　　　　　　　　　　Trinity House, London, 23 November 1872.

Adverting to the further interview with which the Elder Brethren were favoured by a deputation from the Irish Lights Commissioners on the 16th instant, I am directed to acquaint you that, assuming the enjoined particulars of the agreements then arrived at to be correct, this Board will have great pleasure in awarding their statutory sanction in due course.

That the light at Roche's Point, already determined on as dioptric white, and produced from gas, should be fixed, and its distinctiveness secured, if the surrounding rocks will admit of it, by a second light, shown from a window in the tower, at 30 to 40 feet below the present one.

I am, &c.

The Secretary, Irish Lights Office.　　　　(signed)　　Robin Allen.

Enclosure 3, in No. 44.

Irish Lights Office, Dublin,
30 November 1872.

Sir,

With reference to the recent conferences a deputation from the Commissioners of Irish Lights had the honour of having with the Deputy Master and Elder Brethren of the Trinity House on the 15th and 16th instant, and in accordance with your letters of the 13th and 23rd instant, submitted to the Board at their meeting on yesterday, I have to report the statutory sanction of the Trinity House to the several proposed works and changes embodied in said letters.

I also enclose, for the information of the Elder Brethren, copy of letters received from the undermentioned parties on subject of the proposal of your Board of the 3rd October, and which was forwarded by the Board of Trade to this department on the 11th instant, copies having been sent to the parties for any observations they might wish to offer thereon.

Liverpool Shipowners' Association, 4th November 1872 ; Liverpool Steam Shipowners' Association, 5th November 1872 ; Cork Harbour Commissioners, 14th November 1872.

I am, &c.

The Secretary, Trinity House, London.　　　(signed)　　W. Lees.

Enclosure 4, in No. 44.

Sir,   Trinity House, London, 4 December 1872.

I am directed to acknowledge receipt of your letter dated 30th ultimo, adverting to the proposed works and changes which were agreed upon at the recent conference between a deputation from the Irish Light Commissioners and the Elder Brethren of this Corporation, and requesting statutory sanction to the several proposals as embodied in my letters of the 13th and 24th ultimo, as follows, viz.:—

1st. For the better marking of the approaches to Cork Harbour.

A light-vessel outside the Daunt's Rock to show red revolving, and to be fitted with a powerful fog trumpet; a powerful fog trumpet on Poer Head, and a third or a large bell at Roche's Point.

The Roche's Point Light (at present red revolving) to be changed to a fixed white dioptric produced from gas, with a screed light to be shown (providing the surrounding rocks will admit of it) from a window in the tower 30 or 40 feet below the present one.

The light on the Old Head of Kinsale to be improved by the substitution of gas for oil.

2nd. As respects other lights.

          *   *   *   *   *   *   *

In reply, I am now to state that the Elder Brethren approve these changes, &c. as enumerated above, and hereby notify their statutory sanction to the same, subject, as respect the Cork Harbour question, to the satisfactory settlement of financial arrangements.

I am further to state, with reference to that part of the correspondence from the Liverpool Shipowners' Association and the Cork Harbour Commissioners, forwarded in your letter of the 24th ultimo, which relates to the fog signal system on the south and east coasts, that there had been some idea that a signal at the Fastnet was to be preferred to one at Kinsale, but that as the difficulties of establishing a powerful trumpet at Fastnet would be very great, the Elder Brethren will be prepared to consider the alternative of Kinsale when the arrangements are more advanced; and as respect the observations in the same correspondence, as to the fact from which the expenses for the improvements in the neighbourhood of Cork Harbour should be provided, the Elder Brethren have already expressed opinions relative thereto in my letter to the Board of Trade, dated 3rd October last, with copy of which it would appear that you were furnished by that department on the 11th of the same month; and I am now only to repeat that they have accorded their statutory sanction to these improvements, on the distinct understanding that an adequate toll be levied in such manner as may be hereafter determined to meet the expenditure, suggesting finally that the Board of Trade should be furnished by you, for their guidance in this matter, with the number and tonnage of vessels to whom these improvements will be of undoubted value; although if there be no misunderstanding as to the alleged facts that vessels entering Queenstown already pay to the Harbour Commissioners 3,000 l. or 4,000 l. yearly, for which they receive no benefit, &c., it may also be expedient to call the attention of the Board of Trade to that circumstance.

I am, &c.
(signed)   Robin Allen.

— No. 44. —

Commissioners of Irish Lights to Board of Trade.

(H. 5208.)   Irish Lights Office, Westmoreland-street,
Sir,   Dublin, 6 December 1872.

WITH reference to your letter of the 11th October last (H. 4243), forwarding a letter from the Trinity House under date the 3rd of same, relative to the better marking of the approaches to Cork Harbour, I am directed to acquaint you that copies of those documents were transmitted to the Liverpool Shipowners' Association, the Liverpool Steam Shipowners' Association, and the Cork Harbour Commissioners, with the request they would favour this Board with any observations they might wish to make thereon, and I have now the honour to submit, for the information of the Board of Trade, copies of replies received from the several bodies, copies having been also forwarded to the Elder Brethren.

At the suggestion of the Trinity House, a deputation from this Board proceeded to London, and had, on the 12th and 14th ultimo, lengthened interviews with the Elder Brethren in connexion with the important question as to the better marking of the entrance to Cork Harbour; copies of the results arrived at at such interviews, are herewith enclosed.

The statutory sanction of the Trinity House having been requested to the

See Enclosure
in No. 44.

measures embodied in their letters of the 13th and 23rd ultimo, this Board deem it right that the Board of Trade should be so informed.

*   *   *   *   *   *   *

As requested, the enclosure in your letter of the 11th October is herewith returned, a copy being retained in this office.

           I am, &c.

The Assistant Secretary,   (signed)   *W. Lees*, Secretary.
Harbour Department, Board of Trade.

Enclosure 1, in No. 45.

              Shipowners' Association, Liverpool,
              4 November 1872.

Sir,

The Committee for managing the affairs of this association have, at their monthly meeting to-day, taken into consideration your favour of 23rd ultimo, transmitting copies of correspondence from the Board of Trade and Trinity House on the subject of the better marking of the approaches to Cork Harbour; and I am directed to enclose copy of a resolution which this committee arrived at on a former occasion, and to inform you that they have no reason to alter the opinion expressed in that resolution; and that with regard to the proposed payment of the cost and maintenance of the lights, this committee are now in communication with the Government to urge the total abolition of light dues, and they could not under any circumstances agree to the proposal contained in the letter of the Trinity House, dated 3rd ultimo.

           I am, &c.

W. Lees, Esq., Secretary,   (signed)   *Samuel Field*,
Irish Lights Office.   Secretary.

(Copy.)

              Shipowners' Association, Liverpool,
              6 November 1872.

At a Meeting of the Committee held on the 31st July 1872,—

PRESENT:

Mr. Philip Nelson in the Chair, &c. &c. &c.

Approaches to Cork Harbour.—Proposed Fog Signals.

READ, a letter from the Assistant Secretary of the Harbour Department, Board of Trade, stating that a correspondence had lately taken place between the Commissioners of Irish Lights and the Elder Brethren of Trinity House on the subject of the proposal to place a improved fog signal on Roche's Point, and expressing doubt as to the most appropriate position for the establishment of such signals, and requesting this association to transmit any observations they might desire to make on the views expressed as to the situation of it.

It was Resolved, That in the opinion of this association, it would be very advisable that efficient fog signals should be placed on the promontories both to the eastward and westward of the approach to Cork Harbour; viz., the Old Head of Kinsale to the westward, and Poer Head to the eastward; and this association further suggest that Daunt's Rock should have a light-ship, with a fog bell placed near it, which they think could well be made into a pilot, and (if practicable) a telegraph and postal station.

The secretaries were directed to send a copy of the above resolution to the Board of Trade.

             Extracted from the Proceedings.

           (signed)   *Samuel Field*, Secretary.

Enclosure 2, in No. 45.

The Liverpool Steam Shipowners' Association.

The plan now proposed differs from that suggested by the association in some particulars. With regard to the marking of Daunt's Rock, the association are content to defer to the judgment of your Board and the Trinity House, as to whether a light-ship would be preferable to a lighthouse on the headland above the Rock. The former would, no doubt, be the best if it could be made perfectly safe against danger of drifting.

A powerful fog signal on the light-ship would be no doubt a great benefit, but the association are anxious that the desirability of placing a fog signal of the greatest power on the Old Head of Kinsale may not be lost sight of. They would be very glad to have both signals, but in default of both being provided, it is worthy of consideration whether it is not more important to have one on the Old Head rather than nearer to Roche's Point. The Old Head is the point first made. From thence the course to Queenstown is taken.

With regard to the fund out of which the costs of the lights and signals are to be defrayed, the association feel very strongly that it should not fall on the vessels entering Queenstown. Those vessels already pay to the Cork Harbour Commissioners a revenue of 3,000 l. to 4,000 l. yearly, for which they receive no benefit at all. The Harbour Commissioners have a total income of about 30,000 l. a year. The whole of this income is spent upon improvement in the River Lee and at Cork; and although the calling of Atlantic steamers, which contribute the chief amount of the dues on vessels entering the harbour at Queenstown, has proved very beneficial to all persons interested in the harbour of Cork, yet nothing whatever has been done for their benefit.

The association, therefore, protest most strongly against further dues being levied upon vessels calling at Queenstown to defray the expense of the light and fog signals, and considers that the present fund of the Commissioners should be applied to that object.

;Yours, &c.
(signed) Gray Hill, Secretary.

The Secretary, Irish Lights Office,
Westmoreland-street, Dublin.

Enclosure 2, in No. 45.

Sir,
Cork, 14 November 1872.

WITH reference to your letter dated 23rd ultimo, enclosing copies of correspondence from the Board of Trade and the Elder Brethren of the Trinity House on the better marking of Cork Harbour by means of fog signals, I am directed by this Board to acquaint you, for the information of the Commissioners of Irish Lights, that the letters referred to have been carefully considered by a Committee of this Board in conjunction with the harbour master of the port, and their report does not altogether coincide with the views of the Elder Brethren. The Committee consider that the establishment of three fog signals, as suggested, in such proximity to each other, would greatly embarrass mariners making for Cork Harbour, and be more calculated to mislead than otherwise, consequent upon the difficulty there would be in distinguishing one from the other. It is the opinion of the Committee, which has been sanctioned by the Board, that great benefit would be afforded to shipping generally were a light-ship placed to the southward of Daunt's Rock, having a powerful steam fog signal on board; a large piece of ordnance placed on Roche's Point, which could be fixed to times of fogs, and a fog signal on the Old Head of Kinsale. The Board consider these signals and the light-ships would thoroughly and efficiently mark the harbour, and enable the mariner to ascertain his position when on the coast.

With reference to that portion of the correspondence relating to the maintenance of the signals and the manner in which the finances for such are to be raised, the Commissioners desire to state that as this is a matter of Imperial import, they do not consider a local tax ought to be imposed on vessels frequenting the port of Cork.

I have, &c.
(signed) William Dempsey,
Secretary.

William Lees, Esq., Secretary,
Commissioners of Irish Lights.

— No. 46. —

Board of Trade to Trinity House.

Board of Trade, Harbour Department,
Whitehall Gardens, 24 December 1872.

(H. 5209.)

Sir,
I AM directed by the Board of Trade to acknowledge the receipt of your letter of the 6th instant, in which, with reference to previous correspondence, and more particularly to their letter of the 11th October last (H. 4943), on the subject of marking the approaches to Cork Harbour, you state that a deputation on the

subject from the Commissioners of Irish Lights with their Secretary met the Elder Brethren of the Trinity House on the 12th ultimo, and again on the 15th ultimo.

You also transmit the correspondence which has taken place consequent upon that deputation, from which it appears that a definite proposal for the marking of Cork Harbour has, conditionally on a satisfactory settlement of the financial question, received the statutory sanction of the Corporation, and that several other alterations, as enumerated therein, have also received their formal sanction.

In reply to that portion of the correspondence respecting the arrangement for marking the entrance to Cork Harbour, to which the Corporation have conditionally conveyed their statutory sanction, I am to state, with respect to the proposal to place a light-vessel off Daunt's Rock, that in the opinion of Admiral Bedford, one of the professional officers of the Board, it is very uncertain whether a light-vessel would maintain its position there; and I am to request that further consideration may be given to this part of the question, for where, as in the present case, the traffic is so enormous, any uncertainty on the point most involve serious consequences.

So far as is known at present, the bottom in the vicinity of Daunt's Rock does not promise good holding ground, and if the Coningbeg light-vessel occasionally drifts, much more might one in the proposed position be likely to part; and should this happen, then there would be Kinsale Head and Roche's Point lights exhibiting the same characteristics, viz.: powerful fixed gas lights, the only distinction being a lower light shown from a window in Roche's Point Tower, whose range will probably be considerably less than that of the upper light, and invisible at times. The consequence of this might be a liability to mislead, when ships uncertain of their position should make this part of the coast.

But assuming the permanence of the Daunt light-vessel, the question arises whether it is necessary to incur the expense of a 1st order dioptric light at Roche's Point, distant only about four miles from the Rock, and with the powerful lights at Ballycotton and Kinsale Head on either hand.

When all these lights become invisible to guide ships towards the mouth of Cork Harbour, they would have to depend upon the fog signals, and it was principally with reference to the better marking by fog signals that the present discussion originated.

I am also to point out that the fog signals proposed to be placed at Poer Head and Daunt Rock light-vessel, which will be only six miles apart, are to be distinguished merely by intervals of blast, whilst the Board of Trade are advised that it might be more desirable that the sounds as well as the intervals should be different.

I am to add that as at present advised the Board of Trade are disposed to think that any outlay at Kinsale Head should be charged to the passing trade.

A separate communication will be addressed to the corporation respecting the other matters referred to in your letter.

The Secretary, Trinity House.

I am, &c.
(signed)   C. Cecil Trevor.

— No. 47 —

Commissioners of Irish Lights to Board of Trade.

(H. 239.)

Irish Lights Office, Westmoreland-street, Dublin, 13 January 1878.

Sir,
With reference to the subject of the better marking the approaches to Cork Harbour, I am to acquaint you that the Trinity House having in their letter of the 6th December last requested this Board to furnish, for the guidance of vessels to whom these improvements will be of undoubted value, although if there be misunderstanding as to the alleged facts that "Vessels entering Queenstown already pay to the Cork Harbour Commissioners 3,000 l. or 4,000 l. yearly, for which they receive no benefit, &c., &c." (as stated in letter from Liverpool

Liverpool Steam Shipowners' Association of 6th November, copy of which was forwarded on the 6th December to the Board of Trade); I have now to enclose copy of a Return from the Collector at Cork bearing on the subject, which I have to request you will be so good as to submit to their Lordships.

I am, &c.

The Assistant Secretary, (signed) W. Lees, Secretary.
Harbour Department, Board of Trade.

Enclosure in No. 47.

Sir, 7 January 1873.

I have only this morning received the enclosed Return.
Vessels entering Queenstown paid the Harbour Commissioners from August 1872 to August 1873, 2,733 l. 14s. 6d.

I am, &c.

William Lees, Esq., (signed) Arthur Stewart.
&c. &c. &c.

QUEENSTOWN STATION.

6 January 1873.

A RETURN of the Number and Tonnage of Steam and Sailing Vessels calling at or off Queenstown for Orders, or for Receiving or Landing Mails or Passengers, and of Shipping entering the Port for Local Trade, for Year ended 31st December 1872:—

Vessels calling at or off Queenstown for Orders.				For Receiving or Landing Mails or Passengers.				Shipping entering Queenstown for Local Trade.			
Steam.		Sailing.		Steam.		Sailing.		Steam.		Sailing.	
No.	Tons.	No.	Tons.	No.	Tons.	No.	Tons.	No.	Tons.	No.	Tons.
13	6,554	1,441	603,860	646	1,613,809	-	NIL.	-	NIL.	50	8,516

(signed) J. Carragh.

— No. 48. —

Trinity House to Board of Trade.

(H. 1212.)

Trinity House, London, E.C.,
Sir, 1 March 1873.

I am directed by the Board to acknowledge the receipt of your letter (H. 5209), dated 24th December last, requesting re-consideration of certain points in recent proposals for better marking the approaches to Cork Harbour, stating that in the opinion of Admiral Bedford it is very uncertain whether a light-vessel would maintain its position off Daunt's Rock, and also suggesting whether a distinction in sound, as well as in interval, should not be adopted in the proposed fog signals.

In reply thereto I am to acquaint you that the Elder Brethren do not consider the drifting of the Coningbeg light-vessel to give an argument of serious weight against the probable safe riding of one off Daunt's Rock, inasmuch as the accident may probably be attributable to insufficient scope of cable, rather than to bad holding ground, and that the Board having again carefully examined the chart, and finding no rocky bottom laid down in any direction but that of E. by S., at about one mile distant from the Rock, have no reason to doubt that

a suitable

a suitable spot might be found where the vessel could be securely moored. The situation is not so exposed, nor is the holding ground worse than that of many of our light-vessels on the English Coast, and when it is considered that the latter have (by God's blessing) kept their stations through the recent gales, and through those of many past winters, the Elder Brethren do not think that in the case now under question any greater degree of risk is to be apprehended.

If the objection of insecurity be thus reduced to a minimum, that which relates to the errors probably consequent on breaking adrift is to the same extent disposed of, but the Elder Brethren fully concurring in the necessity for caution, as expressed by Admiral Bedford, would agree to make an alternative recommendation as to the lights on Roche's Point, and on the proposed light-vessel, making the latter a powerful fixed red light, which, in that position, will be sufficient for the purpose, and leaving the former as it is at present, viz., red revolving, with the lower light fixed white. The distinction between it and Kinsale will thus be preserved, and the mark for Daunt's Rock from Roche's Point will still remain in case of accident to the light-vessel. With regard to the proposal that the lights at each of those stations may be strengthened, the Elder Brethren, having regard to the valuable trade affected, still concur in the opinion, but they consider that Roche's Point need not be of greater power than 2nd order dioptric.

Referring now to that part of your letter which suggests distinction in sound of fog signals, I am directed to acquaint you that from experience gained in America, the Elder Brethren do not venture yet, so far as regards whistles and trumpets to rely on difference of sound as a means of distinguishing fog signals. It appears to them that guns, bells, or horns, are sufficiently distinct in character for the purpose, but air-horns, syrens, and steam-whistles, when pitched at the low key, most favourable for the travelling of sound, all emit a sound so nearly the same (note for note) as to render it imprudent to rely on distinction between one and the other in arranging a series of signals, and that length of blast and interval alone give sufficient and sure means of identification.

Guided by those considerations the Elder Brethren are of opinion that the approaches to Cork Harbour from eastward or westward will be effectively guarded during fog by powerful air-trumpets on Poor Head and the vessel of Daunt's Rock, with unmistakeably different intervals of blast; and that after having passed either of these signals, vessels will be so far warned that a large bell at Roche's Point will be found sufficient to carry them into the harbour.

With reference to your observation, that as at present advised the Board of Trade are disposed to think that any outlay at Kinsale Head should be charged on the passing trade, I am to state that the Elder Brethren concur therein, and have reason to believe that the Irish Commissioners agree with them.

I am, &c.
(signed)   Robin Allen.

The Assistant Secretary,
Harbour Department, Board of Trade.

— No 40. —

Board of Trade to Trinity House.

(H. 1212.)

Board of Trade, Harbour Department,
Whitehall Gardens, 10 March 1873.

Sir,

With reference to your letter of the 1st instant, further as to the marking of the entrance to Cork Harbour, I am directed by the Board of Trade to state, for the information of the Elder Brethren of the Trinity House, that they would be glad to know whether the Commissioners of Irish Lights concur in the suggestions and recommendations contained therein.

I am at the same time to transmit to you copy of a letter, and its enclosures, which have been received from the Commissioners of Irish Lights, showing the number and tonnage of vessels entering Cork Harbour, which has been furnished to them in accordance with the suggestion contained in your letter to the Commissioners missionary of the 6th December last, copy of which was transmitted to this Board in the communication from the Trinity House of the same date.

I am, &c.

The Secretary, Trinity House. (signed) C. Cecil Trevor.

— No. 50. —

Trinity House to Board of Trade.

(R. 1494.)

Trinity House, London, E.C.,
14 March 1878.

Sir,

I am directed to acknowledge receipt of your letter dated 10th instant (H. 1919), inquiring, with reference to mine of the 1st, upon the subject of the better marking of the approaches to Cork Harbour, whether the Irish Commissioners concur in the suggestions contained therein, and, in reply thereto, I am to enclose the subjoined extracts from a letter from the Irish Commissioners, in which they intimated their concurrence, and to state that they have since undertaken to make a survey of the ground outside Daunt's Rock.

As respects the enclosures in your letter relating to the probable revenue from vessels calling or landing mails and passengers, it will be perceived from the enclosed statement that with the usual oversea tolls of 3-10th of a penny, and the existing abatement, the annual result would be a little under 800 L., and if the Board of Trade in due course should desire the opinion of the Elder Brethren as to the manner in which this amount can be increased to an adequate revenue, they will be happy to consider that question.

As respects the amount received by the Cork Harbour Commissioners, the Elder Brethren have no means of knowing under what plea they are levied, or whether they would in any way be applicable.

I am, &c.

The Assistant Secretary, (signed) Robin Allen.
Harbour Department, Board of Trade.

Enclosure 1, in No. 50.

Extract referred to.

"I have, in reply, to acquaint you the Commissioners concur in the proposed modified charges for marking the approaches to Cork Harbour, as suggested in the draft letter to the Board of Trade.

"Admiral Bedford having expressed a doubt as to whether a light-vessel would maintain its position off Daunt's Rock, and as the Elder Brethren are aware that this Board had originally the same doubts, but, in deference to their opinion, agreed to a light-vessel to mark that danger, instead of a lighthouse on Roberts' Head, the Commissioners, before any final decision is arrived at, suggest the advisability of having the locality accurately surveyed. This Board have written to Captain Sheppard, late Master in the Indian Navy, who has been coastguard officer at Roberts' Cove station for nearly four years, asking whether, in his opinion, a light-vessel could be safely moored off Daunt's Rock, and they now enclose copy of his reply."

Copy of Captain Sheppard's Reply.

"It is my opinion that no vessel could ride out the weather that I have seen during the time I was at the Roberts' Cove station, nearly four years, off Daunt's Rock. I do not know what the holding ground is outside the rock, but my impression is, it is foul between it and the mainland."

Enclosure 2, in No. 50.

Statement referred to.

Vessels calling at or off Queenstown for orders :

				£	s.	d.
Steam, 8,564 tons, at ¼d. per ton, less 66 per cent.	-	-	-	3	-	1
Sailing, 680,180 " "	-	-	-	816	11	6
For receiving or landing mails or passengers :						
Steam, 1,816,028 tons, at ¼d. per ton, less 66 per cent.	-	-	640	11	-	
			£.	760	2	8

Trinity House, 14 March 1873.

— No. 51. —

Board of Trade to Trinity House.

(H. 1494.)

                        Board of Trade, Harbour Department,
Sir,   Whitehall Gardens, 24 March 1873.

I am directed by the Board of Trade to acknowledge the receipt of your letter of the 14th instant, further upon the subject of the better marking of the approaches to Cork Harbour, and enclosing extracts from a letter from the Commissioners of Irish Lights, together with a statement showing the probable revenue from vessels calling, or landing mails and passengers at or off Queenstown.

Since my letter of the 10th instant Admiral Bedford has (with reference to Captain Shephard's opinion, quoted in the extracts from the letter from the Commissioners of Irish Lights) procured from the Admiralty a tracing taken from the original Admiralty Survey.

I now enclose the tracing in question, in order that it may be seen by the Corporation before any final steps are taken in the matter.

The Board of Trade, in sending the tracing, do so purely from a wish that all the information accessible to them should be at the service of the Corporation, and not from any desire to re-open the question.

                                       I am, &c.
The Secretary, Trinity House.   (signed)   C. Cecil Trevor.

— No. 52. —

Mr. Murphy, M.P., to Board of Trade.

(E. 3488.)

Sir,   Sydney-place, Cork, 28 June 1873.

It would be a matter of great importance to the Transatlantic, as well as the general shipping and mercantile interests of the United Kingdom, and also of peculiar concern to the Port of Cork, that the necessary measures should be adopted without delay, to carry into effect the decision, which it is understood has been arrived at, of having the fog-signal system established at some convenient point at Cork Harbour. It is, I believe, quite unnecessary for me to urge upon the Board the pressing necessity of having this arrangement carried out as soon as practicable; but I may mention that within the last few days, owing to its non-existence, a large Transatlantic steamer, as well as other vessels, were delayed for several hours off the harbour.

In connection with the subject, it is perhaps right that I should call attention to the desirability of not confining the fog signal to the steam vessel alone; that is, if such should be the intention of the authorities. The use of a piece of
                                                           ordnance,

ordnance, as at Holyhead, would be most desirable, as, according to the statement of our most experienced master mariners, the steam fog-whistle would not unfrequently be confounded with those of the steam ships themselves, and therefore the firing of a gun at intervals would render the service more complete and satisfactory.

As the matter is one on which the public mind is much engaged, and in which our port is deeply interested, I venture to ask, if the Board can state, what are the arrangements intended, and when they are likely to be carried out.

I am, &c.

(signed)　　　N. D. Murphy.

The Right Hon. Chichester P. Fortescue, M.P.,
President, Board of Trade, London.

P.S.—As illustrative of the necessity of the proposed system at Cork Harbour, it may be well to state that over two million tons of shipping entered and paid harbour and anchorage dues there in 1872. Of those paying anchorage dues, over 700,000 tons were Transatlantic. This is, of course, irrespective of the millions of tons passing.

— No. 52. —

Mr. *Farrer* to Mr. *Murphy*, M.P.

(H. 3468.)　　　　　　Board of Trade, Whitehall Gardens,
Dear Sir,　　　　　　　　　　3 July 1873.

In Mr. Fortescue's absence at Liverpool, I write in reply to your note* of the 28th June to say that the question of marking or preventing dangers in the approach to Cork is getting to be so large and complicated that it is impossible to decide at once, or to state in short terms what is doing or to be done.

The enclosed précis of the correspondence will show you how the matter stands, but it is not sufficiently complete to be made public at present.

Yours, &c.

N. D. Murphy, Esq., M.P.　　　(signed)　　　T. H. Farrer.

— No. 54. —

Board of Trade to War Office.

(H. 3255.)　　　　　　Board of Trade, Harbour Department,
Sir,　　　　　　　　　　　Whitehall Gardens, 3 July 1873.

With reference to the War Office letter of 16th June 1968, forwarding a report by the Director of the Royal Engineer Establishment at Chatham upon the proposal of a Mr. Hugh Palmer to remove the Daunt Rock at the entrance to Cork Harbour, in which it is suggested that, as a preliminary step, a proper survey of the rock should be made by means of a diving apparatus, I am directed by the Board of Trade to acquaint you that they have been in communication with the Commissioners of Irish Lights and the Elder Brethren of the Trinity House upon the subject of the better marking and lighting of the approaches to Cork Harbour.

Among other questions connected with the scheme now under consideration, the attention of this Board has been directed to the necessity for providing
effectual

* A private note to the President accompanied No. 52.

effectual means for warning vessels coming into proximity with the Daunt Rock; and as it is in contemplation to levy a special toll upon vessels entering Cork and Queenstown Harbours, in order that the local trade may contribute towards the cost of the proposed improvements, the Board of Trade are enabled to reconsider their letter to the War Office of 1st July 1868 (H. 2328), in which they stated that, under the circumstances then present, they were unable to advance money to defray the expense of the survey proposed by the Director of the Royal Engineer Establishment.

It has been proposed that a light-vessel should be fixed at Daunt Rock, and that she should be provided with a powerful fog trumpet; but there appear to be both physical and financial difficulties to be overcome before this proposal can be definitely accepted.

Looking to the great improvements in the power of explosives, and in the manner of using them, which have become known since the above-mentioned correspondence took place, this Board are led to the belief that the removal of Daunt Rock might possibly be now effected at a much less cost than that which would be incurred by marking it permanently with a light-vessel.

I am accordingly to request that in bringing the matter to the notice of Mr. Secretary Cardwell, you will move him to be so good as to favour this Board with his opinion as to whether the improvements in submarine explosives and in the boring of rock, together with the larger experience which the Royal Engineers have acquired in these matters, would not encourage an effort being made to remove Daunt Rock to a depth of at least 30 feet below low-water of spring tides, rather than that the large expense should be incurred of maintaining a light-vessel and powerful fog signal for the express purpose of marking this danger in what cannot be other than an imperfect manner.

Should Mr. Cardwell agree with the views expressed in this letter, the Board of Trade will be glad to receive an estimate of the probable cost of the removal of Daunt Rock in the manner proposed; and in the event of its still being thought necessary to have a preliminary survey, such as suggested in your letter of the 16th June 1868, they would be obliged if you are able to give them an approximate estimate of the total cost of such a survey, inclusive of an appropriate vessel.

	I have, &c.
The Under Secretary of State,	(signed) T. H. Farrer.
War Office.	

— No. 55. —

Trinity House to Board of Trade.

(H. 3697.)

Trinity House, London, E.C.,
11 July 1873.

Sir,

ADVERTING to previous correspondence on the subject of marking the approaches to Cork Harbour, I am directed to transmit for the information of the Board of Trade, the accompanying letter and its enclosures, which has been received from the Commissioners of Irish Lights, showing the result of the soundings which have been taken for the purpose of ascertaining the nature of the holding ground in the neighbourhood of Daunt's Rock; and, presuming any doubts as to the probability of a light-vessel maintaining her position thereat, to be thereby set at rest, I am directed to refer to my letters, dated 1st and 14th March last, for the propositions now before the Board of Trade, as desired by the Irish Commissioners and approved by this Corporation (subject to an adequate provision for maintenance from the trade passing or deriving benefit therefrom), viz.:

(1.) A light-vessel to be placed off Daunt's Rock, showing a powerful fixed red light, and to be fitted with a powerful fog trumpet.

(2.) Roche's

(2.) Roche's Point Light to be as at present, red revolving, but of the second order, with a lower light fixed white.

(3.) A powerful fog trumpet to be placed on Poor Head.

(4.) A large fog bell at Roche's Point; and,

(5.) The light on the Old Head of Kinsale to be improved in power.

I am to request that the enclosures to this letter being in original may be returned.

The Assistant Secretary,
Harbour Department, Board of Trade.

I am, &c.,
(signed)   Robin Allen.

— No. 56. —

War Office to Board of Trade.

(H. 3753.)

Sir,   War Office, 17 July 1873.

I am directed by the Secretary of State for War to acknowledge the receipt of your letter of the 3rd instant (H. 3255), and to acquaint you in reply, for the information of the Board of Trade, that he will communicate farther with you in reference thereto, when he has made full inquiries on the subject of the proposed removal of Daunt's Rock at the entrance of Cork Harbour.

The Secretary, Board of Trade.

I have, &c.
(signed)   H. K. Storks.

-- No. 57. --

Board of Trade to Commissioners of Irish Lights.

(H. 3697.)

Sir,   Board of Trade, Harbour Department,
                        Whitehall Gardens, 19 July 1873.

With reference to previous correspondence on the subject of making the approaches to Cork Harbour, I am directed by the Board of Trade to state that they have been informed by the Elder Brethren of the Trinity House that the Commissioners of Irish Lights concur with the Elder Brethren in recommending the following scheme, viz. :

(1.) A light-vessel to be placed off Daunt's Rock, showing a powerful fixed red light, and to be fitted with a powerful fog trumpet.

(2.) Roche's Point Light to be as at present, red revolving, but of the second order, with a lower light fixed white.

(3.) A powerful fog trumpet to be placed on Poor Head.

(4.) A large fog bell at Roche's Point; and,

(5.) The light on the Old Head of Kinsale to be improved in power.

I am now, therefore, to request that you will move the Commissioners of Irish Lights to favour this Board with a detailed estimate of the cost of each of the first four items of the above proposed scheme; (a) as regards first cost, and also (b) as regards annual maintenance; and that you will also inform this Board of the excess of the revenue at present derived from the toll levied for Roche's Point Light over the present cost of maintenance of that light.

The Secretary,
Commissioners of Irish Lights.

I am, &c.
(signed)   W. R. Malcolm.

— No. 58 —

War Office to Board of Trade.

(H. 4121.)

Sir,   War Office, 9 August 1873.

WITH reference to Mr. Farrer's letter of the 3rd July 1873 (H. 8255), concerning the removal of Daunt's Rock at the entrance of Cork Harbour, I am directed by Mr. Cardwell to acquaint you, for the information of the Board of Trade, that a report has been received from the Commanding Royal Engineer in Ireland, stating that no estimate for removing the rock can be prepared with any certainty till a survey of the rock has been made.

This survey can be performed at the present time of year, at a cost not exceeding 10 *l.* or 12 *l.* for working pay of sappers and contingent expenses, as there is a diving apparatus on the defence works which can be used for this survey, and the Cork Harbour Commissioners have most readily come forward with an offer of the use, free of charge, of a steamer belonging to them for the service.

Should the Board of Trade be prepared to incur this expenditure, Mr. Cardwell will give instructions that the survey may be proceeded with at once, and that on its completion an estimate be submitted for the removal of the rock, when a further communication will be made to you as to the method considered most desirable for carrying out the work.

                          I have, &c.

The Secretary. Board of Trade.   (signed)   B. K. Starks.

— No. 59. —

Board of Trade to War Office.

(H. 4121.)

                 Board of Trade, Harbour Department,

Sir,   Whitehall Gardens, 18 August 1873.

I AM directed by the Board of Trade to acknowledge the receipt of your letter of the 9th instant, on the subject of the removal of Daunt's Rock at the entrance of Cork Harbour, stating that a report has been received from the Commanding Royal Engineer in Ireland, to the effect that no accurate estimate for removing the rock can be prepared until a survey has been made, and intimating that Mr. Secretary Cardwell will be prepared to give the necessary instructions for the survey, on learning that the Board of Trade are willing to incur an expenditure of 10 *l.* or 12 *l.* for the working pay of the sappers and contingent expenses.

The Board of Trade direct me now to state that they are prepared to incur an expenditure in the matter not exceeding 12 *l.*, and I am to request that the necessary instructions for the survey may be given.

                          I have, &c.

The Under Secretary of State,   (signed)   W. R. Malcolm.
     War Office.

— No. 60. —

War Office to Board of Trade.

(H. 4341.)

                     War Office, Pall Mall, S.W.,

Sir,   29 August 1873.

WITH reference to your letter, dated 18th August 1873 (H. 4121), I am directed by the Secretary of State for War to acquaint you, for the information of the Board of Trade, that instructions have been given to the Commanding
                                Royal

Royal Engineer in Ireland, to have the survey of Daunt's Rock, Cork Harbour, at once put in hand, and to furnish a report as to the best means, and cost, of removing the rock.

The Secretary, Board of Trade.

I have, &c.
(signed) *H. K. Storks.*

— No. 61. —

Commissioners of Irish Lights to Board of Trade.

(H. 4606.)

Irish Lights Office, Westmoreland-street,
Sir,   Dublin, 23 September 1873.

WITH reference to your letter of the 19th July last (H. 8697), I am to inform you the Commissioners are not in a position to furnish an accurate estimate for the fog signal on Poor Head, county Cork, until they have received a reply from the Trinity House expressing their opinion as to the most improved description of fog signals for general shipping on result of recent experiments at South Foreland, as alluded to in your letter of 29th July last (H. 8877), in the case of Tuskar Station.

The Assistant Secretary,   I have, &c.
Harbour Department, Board of Trade,   (signed) *W. Lees.*
London.

— No. 62. —

Commissioners of Irish Lights to Board of Trade.

(H. 4755.)

Irish Lights Office, Westmoreland-street,
Sir,   Dublin, 6 October 1873.

WITH reference to your letter of the 19th July last (H. 8697), on subject of the conclusions arrived at by the Elder Brethren of the Trinity House and the Commissioners of Irish Lights, relative to the better marking of the approaches to Cork Harbour, the Board of Trade requesting to be furnished with an estimate of cost, under four headings, for carrying into effect such improvements; I am in reply to forward a report from the Inspector of Lights, with estimate of probable cost of placing a light-ship with fog trumpet on board, to mark the Daunt's Rock; another from the engineer giving probable cost of improving Roche's Point Light, &c., and erecting a fog horn establishment on Poor Head; also a report from the accountant, showing his reasons why the information requested in the concluding paragraph of your letter cannot be complied with.

With reference to the estimate of the Inspector for a duplicate fog trumpet for the light-ship, I am to state the Board do not consider such to be necessary; and they direct me to observe that these estimates must be considered as only approximate.

The Commissioners have received copy of the report of the Committee of the Elder Brethren on result of recent fog signal experiments at South Foreland, and from which it appears these experiments have not been completed, the Elder Brethren stating "that very few definite conclusions have yet been arrived at, and that many points yet remain to be decided."

The Commissioners direct me to request the Board of Trade will sanction their proceeding with the carrying out of the works, and adopting the most approved fog signals as you known, as much delay has already occurred, and as the Cork Harbour Commissioners are pressing for expedition in the matter.

I am, &c.

(signed)   *W. Law*, Secretary.

The Assistant Secretary,
Harbour Department, Board of Trade.

Enclosure 1, in No. 62.

Irish Lights Office, Dublin,
9 September 1872.

Sir,

I beg to submit the undernamed estimate of the cost for a new light-vessel to mark the Daunt's Rock, fitted with a powerful fog trumpet, together with the cost for annual maintenance, as directed per Board's Order of 20th July 1872.

ESTIMATE of the probable Cost of a New Light-vessel fitted with a powerful Fog Trumpet to mark Daunt's Rock:

	Probable Cost
	£ s. d.
1 New light-ship complete - - - - -	7,225 — —
1 New Lantern for ditto - - - - -	375 — —
1 New fog-horn - - - - - -	750 — —
1 Duplicate ditto - - - - -	750 — —
	£ 9,100 — —
Annual maintenance of new light-ship - - -	1,400 — —
Annual maintenance of fog-horn - - -	112 10 —
TOTAL - £ 10,512 10 —

I am, &c.

(signed)   R. H. Hamn,
Inspector of Lights.

The Secretary,
Commissioners of Irish Lights.

Enclosure 2, in No. 62.

Irish Lights Office, Dublin,
1 October 1872.

Sir,

As directed, I beg herewith to submit an approximate estimate of the amount that will be required for the erection of the contemplated fog signals, &c., in connection with Cork Harbour.

The sum for the item of raising the focal height of the light at Roche's Point is based on the supposition that the present tower is strong enough, but if on examination I find such not to be the case, I must submit a design for strengthening the walls, and a separate estimate of the expense.

The Estimate is as follows, viz.:

	£	£
ROCHE'S POINT:		
Second order, Steyrie apparatus (revolving), with lantern complete	2,840	
Raising the focal height 15 feet -	150	
Red glass chimks - - - - -	86	
Temporary lantern - - - - -	135	
Lamps and maintenance of light during change - -	290	
Carriage, erection of new and taking down old lantern apparatus - - -	160	
Erection of gas works - - - - -	2,000	
Dwelling for gasman - - - - -	150	
Large fog bell and machine - - - -	170	6,000
POOR HEAD:		
Fog horn similar to that at Howth Bailey - -	760	
Dwelling for keeper - - - - -	400	
Furniture for ditto - - - - -	83	
Roadway and walling - - - - -	350	1,600
TOTAL - - - £		6,571

DAUNT'S ROCK (CORK HARBOUR).

The lower light at Roche's Point, erected in 1864, is an ordinary argand burner in a 31-inch reflector, the light being reflected through a first order lenticular panel.

The combination might be very much improved by substituting a lenticular mirror and a "two ring" gas burner for the present oil-and-reflector, at a cost of about 40 £ sterling.

I am, &c.

The Secretary,
Commissioners of Irish Lights.

(signed)   John S. Sloane, Engineer.

Enclosure 3, in No. 62.

Irish Lights Office, Westmoreland-street,
Dublin, 12 September 1873.

Sir,

In reference to the letter from the Board of Trade of 12th July last, calling for a statement of the excess of revenue derivable from the Roche's Point Light over the present cost of maintenance, I have to state it is impossible for me to give this information; Roche's Point being a passing light, vessels deriving benefit therefrom, and going to England and Scotland without calling at Cork, pay their dues at port of destination, of which we have no knowledge.

W. Lees, Esq., Secretary.

I am, &c.
(signed)   C. A. Tyacr.

— No. 63. —

Mr. Murphy, M.P., to Board of Trade.

(H. 4852.)

Sir,   6, Sydney-place, Cork, 9 October 1873.

I am to leave to make reference to my letter of 28th June last on this subject, addressed to the President of the Board of Trade, and shall feel obliged by receiving such information as it may be in the power of the Board now to give, touching any decision arrived at for carrying out objects so desirable. The Cork Harbour Commissioners have more than once brought the subject under the notice of the Commissioners of Irish Lights; but it would appear by a communication from the latter Board, under date the 2nd instant, that they are waiting until the Elder Brethren of the Trinity House arrive at some definite conclusion.

But in the meantime surely something might be, and ought to be, done. I would earnestly beg to direct attention of the Board to the absolute necessity of providing, without delay, some temporary fog signal service, in lieu of the fog bell at Roche's Point, which is practically useless. A piece of ordnance is suggested for that purpose to be fired at intervals, a plan which one would suppose there ought to be no great difficulty in carrying out; but whatever is to be done ought, I would submit, to be done quickly, as it is no light matter to learn, comparatively unprotected, over two millions tons of shipping, which annually enter Cork Harbour, besides the millions calling off and passing.

I am, &c.

The Secretary,
Board of Trade, Whitehall.

(signed)   N. D. Murphy.

— No. 64. —

Board of Trade to Mr. Murphy, M.P.

(H. 4852.)

Board of Trade, Harbour Department,
Whitehall Gardens, 16 October 1873.

Sir,

I am directed by the Board of Trade to acknowledge the receipt of your letter of the 9th instant, requesting that you may be supplied with such information as it may be in their power now to give respecting the proposals which have been under consideration for the better marking of the approaches to Cork Harbour.

o.67.   H   In

In reply, I am to acquaint you that the Commissioners of Irish Lights and the Elder Brethren of the Trinity House (whose sanction is, as you are aware, necessary) have recently agreed in recommending that (subject to an adequate provision for maintenance from the trades passing or deriving benefit therefrom) the following improvements should be adopted :—

1. A light-vessel to be placed off Daunt's Rock, showing a powerful fixed red light, and to be fitted with a powerful fog trumpet.

2. Roche's Point Light to be as at present, red revolving, but to be changed from catoptric to dioptric of the second order; a lower light (fixed white) remaining as at present to mark Daunt Rock.

3. A powerful fog trumpet to be placed on Poer Head.

4. A large fog bell at Roche's Point ; and,

5. The light on the Old Head of Kinsale to be increased in power.

The estimates of the cost of carrying out these works have been laid before this department only within the last few days.

The Board of Trade will be prepared to give their statutory sanction to these recommendations being carried out by the Commissioners of Irish Lights as soon as it has been settled whence the necessary funds are to be provided.

The Board are still of opinion, and the Trinity House concurs with them, that the expense of this scheme for marking the entrance of the Harbour of Cork, which is for the benefit of the local trade and of those who use the harbour, should not be borne by the general passing trade of the United Kingdom ; but they would not be disinclined (provided the proposals they are about to make to the Liverpool Association and the local trade are accepted) to allow the cost of the improvements now proposed at the existing lighthouse at Roche's Point, numbered 3 and 4, and at the existing lighthouse at the Old Head of Kinsale, numbered 5, to be made at the expense of the Mercantile Marine Fund.

The Board of Trade accordingly propose to intimate to the Steam Shipowners' Association and the Shipowners' Association at Liverpool, and to the Cork Harbour Commissioners, that if the trade which use the harbour are prepared to pay a due of ½d. per ton (subject to the existing statement) to cover the expense of placing and maintaining a light vessel at Daunt's Rock, and a fog signal at Poer Head, as proposed in 1 and 3, this Board will forthwith accord their sanction to the new system of marking, which has been agreed to between the two general lighthouse authorities.

I am to add, that the Board of Trade are not the executive in lighthouse matters, and that no delay in dealing with the present proposal is due to them.

I am, &c.,
(signed)   C. Cecil Trevor.

N. D. Murphy, Esq., M.P.,
6, Sydney-place, Cork.

— No. 56. —

Board of Trade to Liverpool Shipowners' Association.

(IL. 4852.)

Board of Trade, Harbour Department,
Whitehall Gardens, 18 October 1874.

Sir,

With reference to my letter to you of 23rd July 1872 (IL. 3100), and to your reply of the 31st July 1872, on the subject of the better marking of the approaches to Cork Harbour, I am directed by the Board of Trade to acquaint you, for the information of the Liverpool Shipowners' Association, that after a careful consideration of the many proposals which have been made, the Commissioners of Irish Lights and the Elder Brethren of the Trinity House (whose sanction, as you are probably aware, is necessary) have recently agreed in recommending that, subject to an adequate provision for maintenance from the trades passing or deriving benefit therefrom, the following improvements should be adopted :—

1. A light-vessel to be placed off Daunt's Rock, showing a powerful fixed red light, and to be fitted with a powerful fog trumpet.

2. Roche's

2. Roche's Point Light to be as at present, red revolving, but to be changed from catoptric to dioptric second order; a lower light (fixed white) remaining as at present, to mark Daunt's Rock.

3. A powerful fog trumpet to be placed on Poer Head.

4. A large fog bell at Roche's Point; and,

5. The light at the Old Head of Kinsale to be improved in power.

The estimates of the cost of executing these works have, within the last few days, been laid before the Board of Trade, who will be prepared to give their statutory sanction to these recommendations being carried out by the Commissioners of Irish Lights as soon as it has been settled whence the necessary funds are to be provided.

In the opinion of this Board, and with them the Corporation of Trinity House concur, the expense of this scheme for marking the entrance of the harbour of Cork, which is for the benefit of the local trade and of those using the harbour, should not be borne by the general passing trade; but the Board of Trade would not be disinclined, provided that the proposals hereinafter contained are agreed to by the trade using the harbour, to allow the cost of the improvements now proposed at the existing lighthouse at Roche's Point, numbered 2 and 4, and at the existing lighthouse at the Old Head of Kinsale, numbered 5, to be made at the expense of the Mercantile Marine Fund.

I am accordingly to intimate to you that if the local trade and the trade using the harbour of Cork are prepared to pay a due of ½d. per ton (subject to the existing abatement) to cover the expense of placing and maintaining a lightvessel at Daunt's Rock, and a fog signal at Poor Head, as proposed in 1 and 3, the Board will forthwith accord their sanction to the new system of marking which has been agreed upon between the two general lighthouse authorities.

I am to request that you will inform me at your early convenience whether the Liverpool Shipowners' Association accede to the above proposal.

A similar letter has this day been addressed to the Liverpool Steam Shipowners' Association and to the Cork Harbour Commissioners.

	I am, &c.
The Secretary,	(signed) C. Cecil Trevor.
The Shipowners' Association, Liverpool.	

— No. 66. —

Board of Trade to Liverpool Steam Shipowners' Association.

(Similar Letter to No. 65.)

— No. 67. —

Board of Trade to Cork Harbour Commissioners.

(Similar Letter to No. 65.)

— No. 68. —

Mr. Murphy, M.P., to Board of Trade.

(H. 4992.)

Sir, 6, Sydney-place, Cork. 22 October 1873.

I am to acknowledge the receipt of your communication of 18th instant (H. 4862), for which I feel much obliged, and I have laid same before the Cork Harbour Commissioners.

In directing the attention of the Board of Trade, as I did in my letter of 9th

O.67. H 2 instant,

instant, to the pressing necessity of providing some temporary fog signal service, I was perfectly aware that the Board were not the executive, but I naturally assumed, if they concurred with me in the propriety of the suggestion made, that some intimation on their part would be likely to set in motion the proper executive department.

I would take leave to add that I never considered any delay which may have arisen in respect of the proposal now under consideration to be attributable to the Board of Trade. On the contrary, I feel bound to say that the only communications I have made to them, namely, 28th June last and 9th instant, have severally met with immediate consideration, and they have promptly afforded me the information at their command.

I am, &c.

(signed)   N. D. *Murphy*.

The Assistant Secretary,
Harbour Department, Board of Trade,
Whitehall Gardens, London.

— No. 69. —

Liverpool Shipowners' Association to Board of Trade.

(H. 5108.)

Shipowners' Association, Liverpool,
30 October 1873.

Sir,

I have the honour to inform you that your letter of the 16th inst. has been under the consideration of the committee for managing the affairs of this Association, and in reply, I beg leave to hand you copy of the resolutions passed on the subject.

I am, &c.

(signed)   *Samuel Field*, Secretary.

The Assistant Secretary,
Harbour Department, Board of Trade,
Whitehall Gardens, S.W.

Enclosure in No. 69.

At a meeting of the committee of the Liverpool Shipowners' Association, held on the 29th October 1873,

Present:—Mr. James Macdonald (in the chair),
&c. &c. &c.

APPROACHES TO CORK HARBOUR.

Read, Letter from the Assistant Secretary, Harbour Department, Board of Trade, on this subject.

And Resolved, That in acceding to the proposal of the Board of Trade rather than that the approaches to the harbour should remain in their present state, the committee would desire to place it upon record that this Association does not in any way alter its views (so often expressed), as to the desirability of the total abolition of light dues.

And the committee consider that the proposed dues of one halfpenny per ton on the local trade, and the trade using the harbour, will be found to be more than is required to cover the expenses of placing and maintaining a light-vessel at Daunt's Rock, and a fog-signal at Poer Head, as proposed in paragraphs 1 and 8 of the above letter.

That, in communicating these resolutions to the Board of Trade, the secretary should remind the Board that this Association, from the nature of its constitution, has no power to bind individual shipowners.

(Extracted from the Proceedings.)

(signed)   *Samuel Field*, Secretary.

— No. 70. —

Cork Harbour Commissioners to Board of Trade.

(H. 3134.)

Sir,   Cork, 1 November 1878.

I am instructed by the Cork Harbour Commissioners to acknowledge receipt of your communication of 16th ult., and to say that the subject-matter shall receive their earliest attention. It is obvious, however, that the questions involved require deliberation, and that whatever be the result arrived at touching the quarter whence the necessary funds for erection and maintenance are to come, a considerable time must elapse before the works can be completed and in operation; in the meantime there exists the most urgent necessity for providing some remedy or safeguard, 1st, against fog; and 2ndly, for an alteration in the movement of the present light at Roche's Point, for which a general call has been made by the master mariners and shipowners. Both these matters can be easily effected, being within the powers of the Irish Lights Commissioners, and paid for already out of existing revenue. They cannot interfere with any of the contemplated new arrangements, and are, I am instructed, ready to be carried out by the Commissioners if sanctioned by the Board of Trade. Instead of the wretched fog-bell, now literally useless, our board propose to substitute a gun; and I am, I believe, warranted in stating that the Commissioners (Irish Lights), whose attention we have drawn to the matter, are prepared, if sanctioned by the Board of Trade, to adopt this plan rather than that of a larger fog-bell, to be erected at a higher elevation, which has been under their consideration. With reference to these points, I am instructed to call the attention of the Board of Trade to the following facts:—

So far back as 1864 a report was made to the Irish Lights Commissioners, founded on one from the masters of steamers and other vessels sailing out of Cork, as to the necessity of a change in the time of revolution of Roche's Light. The matter was referred to Captain Roberts, Inspector of Lights, and that officer made the following recommendation, under date 27th January 1864:—

"I recommend that the suggestions of the masters of steamers sailing out of Cork to make the time of illumination longer, and that of eclipse shorter, should be carried out, which can be done without altering the present period of revolution."

Nothing has been done.

In the summer of 1872 certain propositions were before the authorities, with the view of removing the bell at Roche's Point and substituting therefor a fog-whistle; but as there was reason to believe those propositions would prove imperative, which subsequently turned out to be the case, the Trinity House sanctioned in the meantime, and in order to avoid delay while the propositions referred to were pending, the placing of a first-rate fog-signal at the Point. It would appear, however, that although the necessity for this measure, and a communication to that effect made to this Board by the Irish Lights Commissioners, under date 19th July 1872, was then actually declared, yet, in consequence of a representation made that fog-signals on Roberts' Head and Poer Head, being respectively three and five miles distant, would be better placed, as no doubt they would for the purpose of Transatlantic and passing vessels, the determination so arrived at by the Trinity House, as regards Roche's Point, has been of no avail, and the trade proper of the port has been in the meantime subjected to peril, expense, and delay.

The Cork Harbour Commissioners respectfully ask is this state of things to continue, and cannot the admitted evil be remedied? To that end, therefore, I am instructed to submit to the Board of Trade the two immediate points I have referred to, and to express the anxious desire of my Commissioners that the alterations proposed may be sanctioned without delay, and intimation of same accordingly given to the Commissioners of Irish Lights.

                                                                I have, &c.

                                    (signed)   William Donegan,
        C. Cecil Trevor, Esq.,   Secretary.
Assistant Secretary, Harbour Department,
        Board of Trade.

— No. 71. —

The Liverpool Steam Ship-owners' Association to Board of Trade.

(H. 5182.)

Sir,   Liverpool, 4 November 1873.

I am to acknowledge the receipt of your letter (H. 4852), dated 16th ult., in which you state that the Commissioners of Irish Lights, and the Elder Brethren of the Trinity House, have recently agreed in recommending certain improvements in the light and fog signals on the coast of the south of Ireland, and that the Board of Trade are prepared to give their statutory sanction to those recommendations being carried out, as soon as it is settled from whence the necessary funds are to be provided, and in which you suggest that the cost of the improvements proposed at the existing lighthouses at Roche's Point and the Old Head of Kinsale, should be made at the expense of the Mercantile Marine Fund, if the local trade and the trade using the harbour of Cork are prepared to pay a due of ½ d. per ton (subject to the existing abatement), to cover the expense of placing and maintaining a light vessel at Daunt's Rock and a fog-signal at Poor Head, of the kind which you mention.

I am instructed to say that the Association consider that the expense of these improvements should be borne by the Cork Harbour Commissioners, who have for years derived a large income from the Atlantic vessels calling at Queenstown without applying any portion of that income to the benefit of those vessels.

Rather, however, than lose the benefit of the proposed improvements, the passing steam trade, generally speaking, would be prepared to pay an amount sufficient to provide for a sinking fund, in regard to the cost of erecting and placing the light-vessel and fog-signal in question, and to support the expense of maintaining them, but there is a strong objection felt to paying anything beyond that amount.

The Association are not aware whether the due of ½ d. per ton (subject to the existing abatement), proposed by the Board of Trade, would or would not be in excess of the amount above mentioned.

                            I have, &c.

The Assistant Secretary,   (signed)   *Gray Hill, Secretary.*
Harbour Department, Board of Trade.

— No. 72. —

Board of Trade to Commissioners of Irish Lights.

(H. 5182.)

                    Board of Trade, Harbour Department,
Sir,   Whitehall Gardens, 14 November 1873.

With reference to previous correspondence on the subject of the better marking of the approaches to Cork Harbour, I am directed by the Board of Trade to acquaint you, for the information of the Commissioners of Irish Lights, that they have this day conveyed to the Corporation of Trinity House their statutory sanction to the adoption of the following improvements :—

1. A light vessel to be placed off Daunt's Rock, showing a powerful fixed red light, and to be fitted with a powerful fog trumpet.

2. Roche's Point light to be, as at present, red revolving, but to be changed from catoptric to dioptric of the second order ; a lower light (fixed white) remaining, as at present, to mark Daunt's Bank.

3. A powerful fog trumpet to be placed on Poor Head.

4. A large fog bell at Roche's Point ; and.

5. The light at the Old Head of Kinsale to be increased in power.

                                          This

This sanction has been given subject to the condition that the local trade, and the trade using the harbour of Cork, for whose benefit the proposed improvements will be, are to bear the expense of placing and maintaining the light vessel and fog trumpet at Daunt's Rock, as in 1, and of the fog signal at Poer Head, as in 8. For this purpose it is intended, at the proper time, to obtain an Order in Council authorising the levying of a toll of 1 d. per ton (subject to the existing abatement) upon the trades in question.

Under the above circumstances the Board of Trade see no objection to the proposed improvements at the existing lighthouse at Roche's Point, numbered 3 and 4, and at the existing lighthouse at the Old Head of Kinsale, numbered 5, being made at the expense of the Mercantile Marine Fund.

As regards the cost of executing the above works, I am to state that this Board have considered the estimates, forwarded in your letter to the Department of the 6th ultimo, and I am now to convey to you their sanction to the expenditure of 8,350 l. for the light vessel and fog trumpet, to be placed off Daunt's Rock, being 9,100 l. (the sum estimated by the Inspector of Lights), less 750 l. for a duplicate fog trumpet, which the Commissioners of Irish Lights think unnecessary.

The Board of Trade also sanction the expenditure of 1,588 l. for the erection of a fog trumpet, dwellings, &c., at Poer Head, and of 770 l. for the fog hall and machine at Roche's Point.

Tenders for all the above works should be invited and submitted, together with plans in the usual manner, to this Department.

As regards the alterations in Roche's Point Light, I am to observe that this Board are not at present prepared to sanction the adoption of gas at that station, and I am accordingly to request that you will obtain and submit a new detailed estimate for the alterations there, and that you will also submit an estimate for carrying out the work necessary for the improvement contemplated at the station of the Old Head of Kinsale.

Having regard to the long period which has elapsed since first the question of improving the marking of the approaches to Cork Harbour was raised, the Board of Trade trust that the Commissioners of Irish Lights will use all possible dispatch in carrying out the arrangements now sanctioned.

I am also to enclose, for the consideration of the Commissioners, copy of a letter which has been received from the Cork Harbour Commissioners, who, it will be perceived, suggest that immediate steps should be taken for altering the time of illumination of the light at Roche's Point, and for placing a fog gun there; and at the same time call attention to the recommendations made with regard to that light in the year 1863.   — No. 70.

The Cork Harbour Commissioners have been informed, in reply, that this proposal cannot be considered by the Board of Trade until it has been recommended by the Commissioners of Irish Lights, and sanctioned in the usual manner by the Trinity House. It has also been intimated to them that they appear to be under some misapprehension in stating that "nothing has been done" respecting the late Captain Roberts' recommendation in 1864 that the time of illumination of Roche's Point Light should be altered, inasmuch as, on the 1st March 1865, the Board of Trade communicated to the Dublin Ballast Board their sanction to the expenditure which the Ballast Board had named as necessary for the purpose, and they have every reason to believe that the alteration was promptly carried into effect.

With regard to the remark made by the Cork Harbour Commissioners, to the effect that the proposal to place a first-rate fog signal upon Roche's Point had received the sanction of the Trinity House so early as last year, the Board of Trade have pointed out that that recommendation gave rise to the prolonged correspondence and discussions which have at length, and but recently, terminated in the agreement of the two lighthouse authorities in recommending the scheme which now receives the sanction of this Board.

                                        I am, &c.
                        (signed)   C. Cecil Trevor.

The Secretary,
Commissioners of Irish Lights.

— No. 73. —

Board of Trade to Trinity House.

(H. 5182.)

Board of Trade, Harbour Department,
Whitehall Gardens, 14 November 1878.

Sir,

With reference to previous correspondence on the subject of the better marking of the approaches to Cork Harbour, I am directed by the Board of Trade to convey to you, for the information of the Corporation of Trinity House, their statutory sanction to the adoption of the following improvements:—

1. A light-vessel to be placed off Daunt's Rock, showing a powerful fixed red light, and to be fitted with a powerful fog-trumpet.

2. Roche's Point Light, to be, as at present, red revolving, but to be changed from catoptric to dioptric of the second order; a lower light (fixed white), remaining, as at present, to mark Daunt's Rock.

3. A powerful fog-trumpet to be placed on Poor Head.

4. A large fog-bell at Roche's Point; and,

5. The light at the Old Head of Kinsale to be increased in power.

This sanction is given subject to the condition that the local trade, and the trade using the harbour of Cork, for whose benefit the proposed improvements will be, are to bear the expense of placing and maintaining the light-vessel and fog-trumpet at Daunt's Rock, as in 1, and of the fog-signal at Poor Head, as in 8. For this purpose it is intended, at the proper time, to obtain an Order in Council authorizing the levying of a toll of one halfpenny per ton (subject to the existing abatement) upon the trades in question.

Under the above circumstances, the Board of Trade are no objection to the proposed improvements at the existing lighthouses at Roche's Point, numbered 3 and 4, and at the existing lighthouse at the Old Head of Kinsale, numbered 5, being made at the expense of the Mercantile Marine Fund; and the Commissioners of Irish Lights have been requested to furnish detailed estimates of the works.

I am also to enclose, for the information of the Elder Brethren of the Trinity House, copy of a letter which has been received from the Cork Harbour Commissioners, who, it will be perceived, suggest that immediate steps should be taken for altering the time of illumination of the light at Roche's Point, and for placing a fog-gun there; and at the same time call attention to the recommendations made with regard to that light in the year 1865.

The Cork Harbour Commissioners have been informed in reply, that this proposal cannot be considered by the Board of Trade until it has been recommended by the Commissioners of Irish Lights, and sanctioned in the usual manner by the Trinity House. It has also been intimated to them that they appear to be under some misapprehension in stating that " nothing has been done " respecting the late Captain Roberts' recommendation in 1865 that the time of illumination of Roche's Point Light should be altered, inasmuch as, on the 1st of March 1866, the Board of Trade communicated to the Dublin Ballast Board their sanction to the expenditure which the Ballast Board had named as necessary for the purpose, and they have every reason to believe that the alteration was promptly carried into effect.

With regard to the remark made by the Cork Harbour Commissioners to the effect that the proposal to place a first-rate fog signal upon Roche's Point, had received the sanction of the Trinity House so early as last year, the Board of Trade have pointed out that that recommendation gave rise to the prolonged correspondence and discussions which have at length, and but recently, terminated in the agreement of the two lighthouse authorities in recommending the scheme which now receives the sanction of this Board.

I am, &c.,
(signed)　　C. Cecil Trevor.

The Secretary, Trinity House.

No. 70.

— No. 74. —

Board of Trade to Cork Harbour Commissioners.

(H. 5182.)

Board of Trade, Harbour Department,
Whitehall Gardens, 14 November 1878.

Sir,

I am directed by the Board of Trade to acknowledge the receipt of your letter of the 1st instant, on the subject of the better marking of the approaches to Cork Harbour.

The Board of Trade observe that the Cork Harbour Commissioners, whilst for the present reserving their opinion upon the proposals contained in my letter to you of the 18th ultimo (H. 4852), suggest that immediate steps should be taken for altering the time of illumination of Roche's Point Light, and for placing a fog gun at that Point.

In reply, I am to observe as follows :—

1. The Harbour Commissioners appear to be under some misapprehension as regards the alteration in the time of illumination of Roche's Point Light, when they state, as they do by your letter, that "nothing has been done" respecting the recommendations of the late Captain Roberts to the Dublin Ballast Board in the year 1865.

That recommendation was forwarded to this Department in the usual manner in February 1865, and received the statutory approval of the Board of Trade by a letter addressed to the Dublin Ballast Board on the 1st of March in the same year.

Although, as the Harbour Commissioners may probably be aware, this Board are not the executive in lighthouse matters, and it did not therefore rest with them to carry out the change which they had sanctioned, they have every reason to believe that the change then recommended and sanctioned was promptly effected by the Ballast Board.

2. As regards the suggestion for placing a fog gun at Roche's Point rather than a larger fog bell as at present proposed.

Before the Board of Trade can consider any proposition of the nature advanced in your letter, it will be necessary that both Lighthouse Boards should in the first instance concur in recommending it. If therefore the Commissioners of Irish Lights entertain favourably the suggestions made by the Cork Harbour Commissioners, they will no doubt apply for the statutory approval of the Corporation of Trinity House, and when such approval has been obtained, this Board will be prepared to give the matter their careful consideration.

The Board of Trade are quite aware that as early as last year the Trinity House sanctioned the placing of a fog signal of the most approved kind on Roche's Point, but so many suggestions for the better marking of the approaches to Cork Harbour were then under the consideration of this Department, that it was thought desirable to submit them all at the same time for the opinion of the Elder Brethren, and of the Commissioners of Irish Lights. The result of mature deliberation and much correspondence upon the subject was the scheme laid before this Board by the two lighthouse authorities, and detailed in my letter to you of the 18th ultimo.

As regards the larger scheme set forth in that letter, I am to acquaint you, for the information of the Cork Harbour Commissioners, that the Board of Trade, having received from the Liverpool Shipowners' and Steam Shipowners' Associations (who represent so large a portion of the trade that uses the Harbour) an expression of willingness to contribute towards the expense of the construction and maintenance of the proposed improvements, have decided to approve of that scheme; and have this day intimated to the Trinity House and the Commissioners of Irish Lights their statutory sanction to the proposals set forth in my letter to you of the 18th ultimo, upon the financial conditions therein mentioned; and they will at the proper time submit for Her Majesty's approval a draft Order in Council, authorising the levying of a toll of 1 d. per ton (subject to the existing abatements) on all vessels using the Harbour of Cork.

The Harbour Commissioners will therefore be relieved from the necessity of further considering the proposals made in that letter.

A copy of your letter of the 1st instant has been transmitted both to the Commissioners of Irish Lights and to the Trinity House, and these authorities have been made acquainted with the substance of this communication to you.

                                                    I am, &c.
                                        (signed)   C. Cecil Trevor.
The Secretary, Harbour Commissioners,
    Cork.

_____

— No. 75. —

Board of Trade to Liverpool Shipowners' Association.

(H. 5182.)

                            Board of Trade, Harbour Department,
                                Whitehall Gardens, 14 November 1878.
Sir,
    I am directed by the Board of Trade to acknowledge the receipt of your letter of the 20th ultimo, on the subject of the better marking of the approaches to Cork Harbour; and in reply, I am to acquaint you, for the information of the Liverpool Shipowners' Association, that they have this day conveyed to the Corporation of Trinity House the statutory sanction of this Board to the improvements detailed in my letter to you of the 18th ultimo (H. 4852), upon the conditions therein mentioned, and that it is the intention of this Board to submit at the proper time for Her Majesty's approval, a Draft Order in Council, authorising the levying of a toll of one half-penny per ton (subject to the existing abatement) on all vessels using the Harbour of Cork.

                                                    I am, &c.
                                        (signed)   C. Cecil Trevor.
    The Secretary,
The Shipowners' Association, Liverpool.

_____

— No. 76. —

Board of Trade to Liverpool Steamship Owners' Association.

(Similar Letter to No. 75.)

_____

— No. 77. —

Cork Harbour Commissioners to Board of Trade.

(H. 5484.)

Sir,   Cork, 21 November 1878.
    I am directed to acknowledge the receipt of your communication of 18th instant, intimating that the Board of Trade have granted to the Elder Brethren of the Trinity House, and the Commissioners of Irish Lights, their statutory sanction to erect the fog signals and improve the lights at Roche's Point and the Old Head of Kinsale, as detailed in your letter of the 18th ultimo, and that at the proper time a Draft Order in Council would be submitted to Her Majesty for her approval, authorising the levying of a toll of ½ d. per ton (subject to the existing abatement) on all vessels using Cork Harbour.

    I am to acquaint you, for the information of the Board of Trade, that the Harbour Commissioners consider that the tax referred to will bear heavily, and disproportionably, upon the local trade of this port, and they trust the Board of Trade will reconsider their decision, and devise another means for meeting the financial requirements necessary for establishing and maintaining the signals.

    I am furthermore to state that should the Board of Trade adhere to their decision, so far as the toll of ½ d. per ton is concerned, it will be in direct contravention to the views and wishes of the Harbour Commissioners, and to which I am instructed to state they most respectfully decline giving their assent.

                                                    I have, &c.
                                        (signed)   William Dunegan,
C. Cecil Trevor, Esq.,   Secretary.
Assistant Secretary, Harbour Department,
    Board of Trade, London.

_____

— No. 78 —

Commissioners of Irish Lights to Board of Trade.

(H. 5653.)

Irish Lights Office, Westmoreland-street, Dublin,
1 December 1872.

Sir,

I am instructed by the Commissioners of Irish Lights to acknowledge the receipt of your letter of the 16th ultimo (H. 5152); and at the same time to express their satisfaction at receiving therein the sanction of the Board of Trade to the carrying out, on certain conditions, of the arrangements agreed upon by the Elder Brethren of the Trinity House and this Board, for the better working of the approaches to Cork Harbour, and to state that no delay shall be allowed to take place in submitting plans, and inviting tenders for the execution of the several works, and that the Inspector of Lights and engineer have already been directed to at once submit estimates of cost in detail.

With reference to that part of your letter as to the request of the Cork Harbour Board, that the present period of visibility of the Roche's Point Light may be made longer, I am to observe that, inasmuch as it has been decided to change this light from catoptric to dioptric of the second order, the Commissioners are of opinion the consideration of this application should be deferred until such change has been effected; and with reference to the statement made by that Board, under date the 1st ultimo, that nothing has been done towards carrying out the recommendation made in January 1865, by the late Inspector of Lights, as to increasing the visibility of this light, and which was sanctioned by the Board of Trade on the 1st March 1865, I have to acquaint you, that on the 2nd May 1865, Captain Roberts reported that the change had been carried into effect on the night of the 28th April 1865, and of which circumstance the Cork Harbour Board were duly informed, as will be seen by the enclosed copies of correspondence.

As regards the further proposition of the Cork Harbour Board, that a gun be substituted in lieu of the present bell at this station, I am to inform you the Commissioners are unable, for the reasons already expressed to the Board of Trade, to recommend this change; and I am to remark, that the observation made by the Cork Harbour authorities, that this Board are prepared to adopt the gun, is erroneous, as the Commissioners of Irish Lights fully concur in the desirability of adopting the powerful fog-bell, already sanctioned by their Lordships.

I am, &c.
(signed)   W. Lees,
Secretary.

The Assistant Secretary,
Harbour Department, Board of Trade.

Enclosure 1, in No. 78.

Ballast Office, Dublin, 2 May 1865.

Sir,

I beg to report to the Board that, on the night of the 28th ult., I made a change in the revolving light at Roche's Point (but keeping it the same period of revolution, viz., one minute) by giving a greater continuance of light and less of eclipse, as suggested in the last paragraph of my report on this light of the 17th of January last, and would suggest that the Cork Harbour Commissioners be informed of the change.

I am, &c.
(signed)   E. V. Roberts,
Inspector of Lights.

The Secretary, Commissioners of Irish Lights.

Enclosure 2, in No. 78.

Ballast Office, Dublin, 6 May 1865.

Sir,

I am directed to forward, for the information of the Cork Harbour Commissioners, the enclosed copy of a report from the Inspector of Lights, stating he has made a change to the revolving light at Roche's Point (but keeping it at the same period of revolution), on the night of the 28th ult.

I am, &c.
(signed)   W. Lees, Secretary.

The Secretary,
Cork Harbour Commissioners, Cork.

— No. 79. —

Board of Trade to Cork Harbour Commissioners.

(H. 5653.)

Board of Trade, Harbour Department,
Whitehall Gardens, 9 December 1873.

Sir,

WITH further reference to your letter of the 1st ultimo, and to the suggestions of the Cork Harbour Commissioners as regards the alteration in the periods of light and darkness of Roche's Point Light, and the proposed substitution of a gun for the present fog bell at that station, I am directed by the Board of Trade to transmit herewith, for the information of the Harbour Commissioners, copy of a communication on the subject, which has been received from the Commissioners of Irish Lights, in reply to the letter which is same to you of the 14th ultimo, I informed you had been addressed to that body.

I am, &c.

The Secretary.
Harbour Commissioners, Cork.

(signed)　　C. Cecil Trevor.

— No. 80. —

Cork Steam Packet Company to Board of Trade.

(H. 5704.)

Sir,　　Cork, 2 December 1873.

I AM instructed by my directors to address you on the subject of the suggested charge of ¼ d. per ton on the local shipping of this port to defray expenses of the proposed lights for the exterior approaches to Cork Harbour, and to point out the injustice of such a mode of levying the charge.

The benefit of the light will be chiefly derived by passing vessels and those trading to westward, whereas the tonnage of the steamships represented by this Company, trading to eastward, amounts to over 300,000 tons annually, and on which, though they do not require the light or pass in their regular course within several miles of it, a considerable part of the cost of maintenance will fall.

I have, therefore, respectfully to request that your honourable Board will reconsider the mode of charging the dues for this light, and cause the expenses of maintenance to be levied not on ensuing vessels coming from or going eastwards and engaged in the local trade of Cork, but on those trading to westward and calling at Cork for orders or passengers, and not for the purpose of local trade, such vessels being those desiring or likely to be benefited by the light in question.

I have, &c.

The Right Hon.
Chichester Fortescue, President of the
Board of Trade, London.

(signed)　　George Cotter Beale.

— No. 81. —

Board of Trade to Commissioners of Irish Lights.

(H. 5704.)

Sir,

Board of Trade, Harbour Department,
Whitehall Gardens, 15 December 1873.

I AM directed by the Board of Trade to refer to previous correspondence on the subject of the improvements in the marking of the approaches to the
Harbour

Harbour of Cork, and more particularly to your letter of the 13th January last, which enclosed a return of the number and tonnage of the vessels calling at or off Queenstown or entering the port for the year 1872.

In this return the tonnage of vessels frequenting Cork was distributed as follows :—

	Steam.	Sailing.
	Tons.	Tons.
Vessels calling for orders - - - - - -	8,444	400,550
Steamers receiving or landing passengers or mails	1,615,828	—
Sailing vessels entering Queenstown for purposes of local trade - - - - - -		9,816

I am now to state that communications have been received from the Cork Harbour Commissioners and the City of Cork Steam Packet Company, with reference to the proposed toll of 1 d. per ton on all vessels using the harbour or calling off it, and that the letter of the latter Company states the tonnage of their steamers trading eastward alone at 300,000 tons, while both the above bodies have the impression that the burden of the proposed tax will chiefly fall on the local trade using the harbour, and not on the vessels calling for orders, passengers, or mails.

The Board will be glad to be favoured by the Commissioners of Irish Lights with an explanation of the apparent discrepancy between the statement of the Packet Company respecting the tonnage of their steamers (viz., 800,000 tons), and the tonnage assigned to the local trade in the return (viz., 9,816 tons), and also with any observations they may have to offer as to the principle on which the toll should be levied, and the proportion which should be charged on the several amounts of tonnage recited above, so as to cause each class of trade to pay its fair share of the annual sum of, say, 2,300 L, required to recoup the Mercantile Marine Fund for the first cost and maintenance of part of the proposed improvements, and also as to whether under ordinary circumstances all should be charged in and out, and if not what would be the exceptions.

The Board of Trade will be glad to receive a reply to this letter at the early convenience of the Commissioners of Irish Lights.

The Secretary,
Commissioners of Irish Lights.

I am, &c.
(signed)   C. Cecil Trevor.

— No. 82. —

Board of Trade to Cork Harbour Commissioners.

(H. 5704.)

Board of Trade, Harbour Department,
Whitehall Gardens, 15 December 1872.

Sir,
I am directed by the Board of Trade to acknowledge the receipt of your letter of the 21st ultimo, in which you state, with reference to the proposed toll of ½ d. per ton on the shipping using the Harbour of Cork to provide for a part of the expense of the improvements in the marking of the approaches thereto, that the Harbour Commissioners consider that the tax in question will bear heavily and disproportionally upon the local trade of the port, and urge the reconsideration of the decision arrived at on the point by the Board of Trade.

In reply I am to observe that there would seem to be an imperfect understanding on the part of the Commissioners in the matter of the toll in question, and I am to state that it is proposed to be levied not only upon the local trade, properly so called, but upon all vessels calling for orders, passengers, or mails.

The scheme is essentially one for the benefit of shipping using the harbour

0.67.   I 3   or or calling off it, and must be considered in its entirety and not piecemeal, and it is on this account alone that the Board of Trade have felt themselves justified in departing to some extent from their usual principle in allowing a portion of the expense of improvements required for local wants to be borne by the Mercantile Marine Fund.

No vessels in the local trade ought to be altogether free from contributing to what will have to be raised from local sources towards the cost of the whole scheme.

> I am, &c.
>
> (signed)   C. Cecil Trevor.

The Secretary,
Harbour Commissioners, Cork.

— No. 83. —

Board of Trade to City of Cork Steam Packet Company.

(H. 5704.)

Board of Trade, Harbour Department,
Whitehall Gardens, 15 December 1874.

Sir,

I am directed by the Board of Trade to acknowledge the receipt of your letter of the 2nd instant, relative to the proposed toll of ½ d. per ton on all shipping using the Harbour of Cork, to provide for a part of the expense of the proposed improvements in the marking of the approaches thereto, and to reply to observe, as there seems to be some misunderstanding on this point, that the proposed local toll will be levied not only upon the local trade, properly so called, but upon all vessels calling at Cork for orders, passengers, or mails, and that the scheme is essentially one for the benefit of shipping using the harbour or calling off it.

I am to point out that the proposed fog signal on Poer Head will be of especial use to all vessels, including of course those of your Company, coming from or going towards the east, while the Company's steamers, if not ordinarily, as remarked in your letter, requiring the light vessel at Daunt's Rock, which lies out of their regular course, may nevertheless derive advantage from it in warning them of their danger in cases where they are out of their reckoning, and have overrun their distance in thick weather.

The scheme must be considered in its entirety and not piecemeal, and on this account alone have the Board of Trade felt themselves justified in departing to some extent from their usual principle, by allowing a portion of the expense of improvements required for local wants to be borne by the Mercantile Marine Fund. No vessels in the local trade ought to be altogether free from contributing to what will have to be raised from local sources towards the cost of the whole scheme.

> I am, &c.
>
> (signed)   C. Cecil Trevor.

The Secretary,
City of Cork Steam Packet Company, Cork.

— No. 84. —

Commissioners of Irish Lights to Board of Trade.

(H. 5929.)

Irish Lights Office, Westmoreland-street,
Dublin, 19 December 1876.

Sir,

I am directed by the Commissioners of Irish Lights to acknowledge the receipt of your letter of the 15th December (H. 5704), on subject of the return of the tonnage frequenting Cork Harbour, as forwarded in my letter of the 13th January last, and in reply, to state, the Commissioners furnished the Board of Trade with a copy of the return as given to them by the Collector of Customs, Queenstown; the Collector has, however, been again written to for

for an amended statement, the Commissioners believing that the return already received only contained the tonnage of vessels using Queenstown, and not that of the vessels proceeding up to Cork.

I am to add, the Commissioners will give the other matters contained in your letter their immediate attention, and will communicate their opinion without delay.

	I am, &c.
The Assistant Secretary,	(signed) W. Lees, Secretary.
Harbour Department, Board of Trade.	

— No. 85. —

Cork Harbour Commissioners to Board of Trade.

(H. 6018.)

Sir,   Cork, 19 December 1873

THE Cork Harbour Commissioners having had under their further consideration the letter of the Board of Trade of 11th ultimo, as well as that of the 9th instant, since received, I am directed by them to submit the following observations, in addition to those contained in my communication of 21st ultimo.

(1.) With respect to the alteration in the time of illumination of Roche's Point Light.

You observe in yours of 14th ultimo that the Cork Harbour Commissioners appear to be under some misapprehension as regards the time of illumination, when they state that "nothing" has been done respecting "the recommendation of the late Captain Roberts to the Dublin Ballast Board in the year 1865," and you further observe that the "recommendation was forwarded in February 1865 to the Board of Trade, and received their statutory sanction, and (as they had reason to believe) that the change then recommended and sanctioned was promptly effected." In corroboration of this statement, you send with your letter of 9th instant, copies of letters from the Irish Lights Commissioners, and of the report of the late Captain Roberts purporting to show that the alterations were made.

This statement, raising as it does, a direct issue upon a matter of fact, namely, whether the recommendation of 27th January 1865, referred to by the Cork Harbour Commissioners has or has not been carried out, renders it obligatory on them to state the grounds upon which they made their representation, as well as their reasons for continuing to believe that such representation is substantially correct.

The case stands thus. Prior and up to 1864, Roche's Point Light was a fixed one. It was then altered to one of "six seconds" of illumination, and 54 seconds of eclipse.

In January 1865 the masters of steamers sailing out of the port of Cork addressed a memorial or remonstrance to the Cork Harbour Commissioners, pointing out the inconvenience and danger of this change, and praying that the light should be altered by exactly reversing the period; namely, that the time of illumination should be 54 seconds, and of eclipse, 6.

After stating that in their opinion it was a very unsafe and dangerous description of light to run for, as a harbour light, on a thick or hazy night, with a gale blowing on the coast, and giving very clear and decisive reasons for this opinion, they then say, "In the event of your deciding upon retaining a revolving light, we would respectfully suggest that the period of illumination and eclipse be reversed; and that its maximum brilliancy be 54 seconds instead of six as at present, so as to allow it to approach as close as possible to a fixed light similar to that which was recently removed."

This memorial, a copy of which I enclose, was forwarded to the Ballast Office, Dublin, on January 1865, and Captain Roberts reported upon it under date 27th January 1865, as follows :—

"In reference to complaints signed by masters of steamers sailing out of port of Cork :

"I think them well deserving the attention of the Board, for the harbour rock inside Roche's Point obliges vessels running in for the harbour to hug the
0.67.   I 4   point

point closer than would be otherwise necessary, in order to avoid it ; and with a following sea a vessel is very likely to yaw considerably, and this might happen when close to the Point, and *the light at the same time in its revolution achieved, when the helmsman losing sight of it, would have nothing to guide him in checking her yawing, except the compass, which might not act sufficiently quick at the critical moment, when so close to the danger.*

"*I therefore recommend their suggestion* (to make the time of illumination longer and that of eclipse shorter), *should be carried out*, which can be done without altering the present period of revolution."

I am to observe this is the recommendation the Commissioners referred to in their letter of 1st ultimo, accompanied by a copy of this last paragraph.

To anyone reading this report in its ordinary and natural sense, it would appear that the suggestions of the masters of steamers were approved of and recommended to be carried out ; yet there the matter remains, substantially to this moment, and the masters of vessels have been frequently complaining of the danger. I am further to observe that the Cork Harbour Commissioners, under date 19th July last, again directed the attention of the Irish Lights Commissioners to the subject, and it was therefore with no small surprise they learned in reply to their further application of 1st instant to the Board of Trade, that "the recommendation of the late Captain Roberts to the Dublin Ballast Board in the year 1863, was forwarded to the Board of Trade in February 1865, had received their statutory sanction on 1st March in some year, and had been promptly effected."

What this recommendation so forwarded was, the Cork Harbour Commissioners are ignorant of ; but presuming it to refer to the change afterwards made from six seconds to ten in the time of illumination of Roche's Light, they scarcely think it possible (having regard to the suggestions of the masters of steamers so approved of) the Board of Trade could have been aware of these suggestions, or that this infinitesimal alteration was all that was desired, or was requisite, when they pointed out that the Cork Harbour Commissioners were under a misapprehension. Indeed, from the complete absence of any statement throughout the entire correspondence enclosed in your letter of the 9th instant as to the nature and extent of this alteration, they are inclined to come to this conclusion. Unexplained, the correspondence would lead to the inevitable inference that the requirements of the masters had been carried out, and, therefore, that the representations of this Board were groundless and uncalled for. But what is the fact ? The masters of steamers suggested that 54 seconds of illumination should be given instead of six. The Inspector of Lights, so far as the language of his report may be naturally interpreted, approved of this suggestion. *Four seconds* only, in addition to the existing *six*, were given, instead of 54 ; and so far as the object sought to be attained was concerned, that is, the reversal of the period of illumination, the change must be considered as practically nil. Under these circumstances, the Cork Harbour Commissioners consider they were substantially, although not, perhaps, literally correct when they observed that "nothing" had been done.

They may not unfairly aver, however, that next to nothing has been done, and they venture again respectfully to draw the attention of the Board of Trade to the subject.

While fully aware that the Board are not the executive in these matters, they at the same time apprehend that, without their sanction or instance, the proper executive cannot be set in motion. They do not now desire to make further reference to the delay which has taken place, or to enter into its causes. It may be that the structural nature of the light did not permit the necessary alterations to be made ; but now that it has been decided on to alter the character of Roche's Light, they trust that the required change in the period of illumination, so long desired, may at the same time be effected.

Compelled, as they have been by the nature of your reference to this subject, to enter into this lengthened statement, they at the same time do not regret the circumstance, as no room for doubt can now remain both as to the reasonableness of their request and the urgent necessity for its adoption.

2. With respect to the proposed toll of ½ *d*.

The Cork Harbour Commissioners would again beg the Board of Trade to reconsider this question so far as affects the local trade of the port of Cork. In your

your letter of 18th October ultimo, one of the reasons assigned for the proposed imposition on that trade, was that the intended expenditure (which they believe in the main is conversant with Daunt's Rock and the Old Head of Kinsale Light) would be for the benefit of (and would consequently tend to improve) the local trade. We beg to point out that this is not the case. The greatest proportion of the local trade is carried on in vessels whose track is several miles from, and altogether away from, Daunt's Rock or the Old Head. On the other hand, there is no question of the great advantage which this light will afford to the Transatlantic steamers in enabling them to keep on their speed in approaching Cork Harbour from the westward, and it is fairly due to them that this additional safeguard should be provided. But permit me to illustrate the effect of this proposed tax in its extreme unequal incidence on the local trade as contrasted with oversea vessels. I shall take, say, a regular trading Cork steamer of 1,000 tons, and compare its contribution to the tax with 1,000 tons of a regular Transatlantic steamship. The Cork steamer makes its average voyage in and out twice a week, or say 104 times a year. The Transatlantic steamer makes its voyage say, twice a month, or 24 times in the year, so that by the measure proposed every ton of Cork shipping contributes over four times the amount that a ton of Transatlantic shipping does. And for what would this be? For the almost exclusive benefit of the latter, as well as other oversea vessels coming from the westward. Again, what is the difference of contribution to the Cork Harbour dues between those two classes? Every ton of shipping engaged in the Cork trade pays a tonnage due of 3 d. over and besides an import and export due on cargo or merchandise except colliers, which pay 2 d. On the other hand, the Transatlantic steamer pays but 1 d. per ton, which includes the return voyage, or say ½ d. per ton for each, and they, as well as all other vessels not discharging or receiving cargo, can use Cork Harbour without any limit as to time, or without any payment to the Commissioners than this ½ d. per ton. Considering that very large portion of the trade enjoyed by those steamers in their peculiar traffic, i.e., the transport of emigrants, an immense proportion of which is effected in the port of Cork, their taxation, than locally understood, contrasts very favourably with that of the Cork shipping. But on this head the Commissioners do not found any complaint; they merely refer to it by way of contrast, and as an illustration of the argument in hand. I am, however, to observe that the trade of Cork does not derive any benefit from those vessels. They neither import nor export merchandise, and while the Commissioners think it a grievance that their local trade should be, as it were, exceptionally taxed for a light not required by them, they at the same time would suggest, if any local additional tax must be imposed (which, however, they protest against), it should be on the principle which regulates the payment of the passing lights dues as between coasters and oversea vessels. Daunt's Rock and the Old Head are several miles from Cork Harbour.

Looking, however, to the nature of the postal and international communication involved in the Transatlantic steamship service, the Commissioners venture to express it as their opinion that the expense of better marking the approaches to Cork Harbour from the westward, as now proposed, while for the almost exclusive benefit of that service, should nevertheless be considered rather as an item of imperial concern, or one to be borne out of the general lights revenue or Mercantile Marine Fund, than one calling for the taxation of the trade and shipping of Cork.

<table>
<tr><td>To the Assistant Secretary,
Harbour Department, Board of Trade,
Whitehall, London, S.W.</td><td>I have, &c.
(signed)   William Donegan,
Secretary.</td></tr>
</table>

P.S.—The Commissioners observe that their proposal to substitute a gun in lieu of the present useless fog bell at Roche's Point, has been rejected. This proposal was made at the instance of the master mariners, who day and night throughout the year sail to and out of the harbour, and whose opinion, it appears to them, should therefore be entitled to some consideration. They trust, however, that the " powerful fog bell " which they are informed the Irish Lights Commissioners have determined on, may, when erected, prove efficacious.

With reference to what the Irish Lights Commissioners, in their letter of the 1st instant, state to be the erroneous observation made by this Board, namely, that

0.67.   K

that they, the Irish Lights Commissioners, would be prepared to adopt the gun, the Cork Harbour Commissioners beg to refer to their letter of 1st ultimo, in which they do not state this as a matter of fact, but only express their belief that such would be the case, provided the Board of Trade sanctioned the change, and they were led to this conclusion by the opinion of their fog signal committee, who conceived they had some reason to express it. However, the matter is of no importance, and they merely advert to it as their attention has been thus called to the subject.

Enclosure in No. 85.

(Similar to Enclosure 0, in No. a.)

— No. 86. —

Commissioners of Irish Lights to Board of Trade.

(H. 6016.)

Irish Lights Office, Westmoreland-street,
Dublin, 20 December 1873.

Sir,

WITH reference to previous correspondence on subject of marking the approaches to Cork Harbour, I am to acquaint you the Commissioners communicated with the Elder Brethren of the Trinity House, with a view to obtaining their opinion as to the most improved light-ship, and most powerful description of fog trumpet, and I am to enclose copy of a reply received under date the 13th instant, and to state the Commissioners think it desirable to await the result of the experiments by the Elder Brethren as to fog signals, but that they are prepared to place a light-vessel off Daunt's Rock at once, should the Board of Trade think it advisable to do so before placing a fog trumpet on board of her.

           I am, &c.

The Assistant Secretary,   (signed)   W. Lees, Secretary.
Harbour Department, Board of Trade, S.W.

Enclosure 1, in No. 86.

Irish Lights Office, Dublin,
1 December 1873.

Sir,

WITH reference to your letter, forwarding drawings and specifications for a wooden light-vessel, of an improved description, in 1851, I am to state that my Board will feel further obliged if the Elder Brethren will favour them with any additional drawings, &c. for the most improved description of light-ship since 1851, and a board which the most improved fog horn has been fitted, with the name of patentee. The above information is solicited, having for its object the placing of a light-ship with powerful fog horn or trumpet, to mark Daunt's Rock. An early reply will much oblige.

           I am, &c.

R. Allen, Esq., Trinity House,   (signed)   W. Lees.
London.

Enclosure 2, in No. 86.

Sir,   Trinity House, London, 13 December 1873.

WITH reference to your letter of 1st instant, I have to state, for the information of the Commissioners of Irish Lights, that the light vessels constructed in recent years for this Corporation Service, were built on the same lines as those in use in 1851, the length only of the vessels having been increased, as explained in my letter of 23nd ultimo.

With regard to the trumpet and fog horn apparatus, which are now in use on board a few of the light-vessels, I have to acquaint you that at the present time the Elder Brethren, with the assistance of Professor Tyndall, have their attention directed to experiments the result of of which will probably lead to the adoption of a more powerful fog signal than either of those now in use. Until the experiments in question have been concluded, the Elder Brethren are not desirous of recommending for adoption by your Board the signals before referred to.

W. Lees, Esq.,
Secretary, Irish Lights Office, Dublin.

I am, &c.
(signed)   Robin Allen.

— No. 87. —

Board of Trade to Commissioners of Irish Lights.

(H. 6018.)

Board of Trade, Harbour Department,
Whitehall Gardens, 29 December 1878.

Sir,

Referring to the previous correspondence on the subject of the proposed improvements in the marking of the approaches to Cork Harbour, and more particularly to your letter of the 1st instant, and mine of the 16th (H. 5704), I am directed by the Board of Trade to transmit herewith, for the information of the Commissioners of Irish Lights, a letter which has been received from the Cork Harbour Commissioners, and I am to request that you will move the Commissioners in replying further to my letter of the 15th instant to favour this Board at their early convenience with their observations on that part of the letter of the Harbour Commissioners which refer to the proposed toll upon the vessels using Cork Harbour.

No. 88.

I am, &c.
(signed)   C. Cecil Trevor.

The Secretary,
Commissioners of Irish Lights.

Part II.

CORRESPONDENCE between the Commissioners of Irish Lights and the Corporation of Trinity House, and the Cork Harbour Commissioners (not included in Part I.)

[As returned by the Commissioners of Irish Lights.]

— No. 88. —

Cork Harbour Commissioners to Dublin Ballast Board.

Cork Harbour Commissioners Office,
Cork, 9 January 1865.

Sir,
By directions of the Cork Harbour Commissioners, I beg to enclose you copies of reports lately made on the additional light at Roche's Point, as also to inquire when the beacon, as recommended by the Board of Trade, will be put on Daunt's Rock.

I am, &c.
To the Secretary,   (signed)   James F. Sugrue,
Ballast Office, Dublin.   Secretary.

Enclosures in No. 88.

(Similar to Enclosures in No. 1.)

— No. 89. —

Dublin Ballast Board to Cork Harbour Commissioners.

Sir,   Ballast Office, Dublin, 12 January 1865.
I am directed to acknowledge the receipt of your letter of the 9th instant, transmitting copies of reports made by the Harbour-masters of Cork and Queenstown, on the additional light from Roche's Point tower to mark Daunt's Rock.

In reply, I am to request you will have the goodness to assure the Cork Harbour Commissioners that the subject shall have the careful consideration of the Board.

With respect to your inquiry when the ball boat sanctioned by the Board of Trade is to be placed to mark Daunt's Rock, I am to acquaint you, for the information of the Commissioners, that tenders have been invited for its construction, to be sent in on or before the 19th instant.

I am, &c.
To the Secretary,   (signed)   W. Lees,
Cork Harbour Commissioners.   Secretary.

— No. 90. —

Dublin Ballast Board to Trinity House.

Sir,   Ballast Office, Dublin, 6 February 1865.
WITH reference to previous correspondence on the subject, I am directed to
forward for the consideration of the Elder Brethren, the enclosed copy of a
report approved by the Board from the Inspector of Lights, Captain Roberts, R.N.,
on the several communications referred to him (copies herewith) relative to the
alteration in Roche's Point Light, and as to the better marking Daunt's Rock.

P. H. Berthon, Esq.,   I am, &c.
Trinity House, London.   (signed)   W. Lees,
                                                                Secretary.

Enclosure in No. 90.

(Similar to Enclosure 1, in No. 6.)

— No. 91. —

Trinity House to Dublin Ballast Board.

                                                  Trinity House, London, E.C.,
Sir,   22 February 1865.
THE Elder Brethren having given attentive consideration to the report of
Captain Roberts, copy of which was transmitted in your letter of the 6th
instant, on the several communications relative to the alteration in the lights at
Roche's Point, copies of which you also transmitted, I am directed to acquaint
you, for the information of the Port of Dublin Corporation, that they concur in
the recommendation of that officer that the period of duration of the light
should be lengthened, and that of the eclipse made shorter.
With respect to the propositions for better defining the exact position of the
Daunt's Rock, I am to state that the Elder Brethren are of opinion that the
present arrangement of the light at Roche's Point, together with the intended
establishment of a bell buoy or boat, are sufficient for the safe navigation of
vessels employed in the passing trade.

The Secretary,   I am, &c.
     Ballast Office, Dublin.   (signed)   P. H. Berthon.

— No. 92. —

Dublin Ballast Board to Cork Harbour Commission.

Sir,   Ballast Office, Dublin, 25 February 1865.
WITH reference to your letters of the 9th and 13th ultimo, transmitting
copies of communications and reports on subject of the present additional light
from Roche's Point Tower to mark the Daunt's Rock, I am directed to forward
herewith copy of the Inspector of Lights report thereon, to whom the documents
0.67.   K 3   were

were referred, and to state that the Board of Trade and Elder Brethren having signified their concurrence in Captain Roberts' recommendations, this Board have directed the same to be carried out.

                                        I am, &c.
                                (signed)   W. Lees, Secretary.
The Secretary,
      Harbour Commissioners, Cork.

Enclosure in No. 92.

(Similar to Enclosure 1, in No. 6.)

— No. 93. —

Dublin Ballast Board to Cork Harbour Commissioners.

Sir,   Ballast Office, Dublin, 20 June 1865.
    I am directed by the Port of Dublin Corporation to forward for the information of the Harbour Commissioners of Cork, the enclosed notice notifying the placing of the bell boat off Daunt's Rock, near Cork Harbour.

                                        I am, &c.
                                (signed)   N. Proud,
Secretary,   Assistant Secretary.
      Cork Harbour Commissioners.

— No. 94. —

Cork Harbour Commissioners to Dublin Ballast Board.

                              Cork Harbour Commissioners Office,
Sir,   Dublin, 22 June 1865.
    Yours of the 20th to hand with notices of the bell buoy at Daunt's Rock, and for which am much obliged.

                                        Yours, &c.
The Secretary, Ballast Office.   (signed)   James P. Sugrue.

— No. 95. —

Commissioners of Irish Lights to Cork Harbour Commissioners.

                                    Irish Lights Office Dublin,
Sir,   30 March 1868.
    I am directed by the Commissioners of Irish Lights to acquaint you that they have for some time past been in communication with the Board of Trade upon the subject of an offer which has been made for the removal of a portion of the Daunt's Rock as is at present dangerous to navigation. In the last letter of the Board of Trade, dated the 25th instant, their Lordships express an opinion that if the attempt be made and prove successful, the Port of Cork and the Post Office authorities should contribute towards the expense. As the correspondence has been considerable, and the verbal explanations given by the proposed contractor to a Deputation of this Board are necessary in order to
                                                              explain

explain more fully the views entertained by this Board upon the matter, I am to suggest whether a personal interview with such of the Cork Harbour Commissioners as they select would not be desirable, and I am to add, that any time that may suit the convenience of the Commissioners, this Board will be happy to meet them here on receiving 24 hours' notice.

I am, &c.

The Secretary, Harbour Board, Cork.   (signed)   W. Lees,
Secretary.

— No. 90.—

Cork Harbour Commissioners to Commissioners of Irish Lights.

(Similar to Enclosure in No. 71.)

— No. 97. —

Commissioners of Irish Lights to Cork Harbour Commissioners.

Irish Lights Office, Dublin,
Sir,   1 June 1868.

Wira reference to previous correspondence, and to your letter of the 2nd April last, relative to the Port of Cork and the Post Office authorities contributing towards the expense of the removal of a portion of Daunt's Rock for the sum named (8,000 L.) in a proposal from Mr. Palmer, I am now directed to transmit, for the information and consideration of the Cork Harbour Commissioners, copy of a letter from my Lords of the Committee of Privy Council for Trade, under date 22nd ultimo, this Board having forwarded to their Lordships copy of your letter referred to above, as also copy of a letter on the subject received in reply from Her Majesty's Postmaster General.

I am, &c.

The Secretary, Harbour Board, Cork.   (signed)   W. Lees.

Enclosure in No. 97.

(Similar to No. 81.)

— No. 98. —

Commissioners of Irish Lights to Cork Harbour Commissioners.

Irish Lights Office, Dublin,
Sir,   20 June 1868.

Wira reference to your letter of the 5th instant, stating that as Daunt's Rock is outside the jurisdiction of the Commissioners of Cork Harbour, the Commissioners will feel bound to resist any toll bring levied on the trade of Cork in furtherance of removing that Rock. I am directed to acquaint you that this Board forwarded a copy of that letter to the Board of Trade, and in reply have received from their Lordships the enclosed letter (copy), which I am to request you will submit to your Commissioners.

I am, &c.

The Secretary,   (signed)   W. Lees,
Harbour Commissioners, Cork.   Secretary.

Enclosure in No. 98.

(Similar to No. 84.)

— No. 99. —

Cork Harbour Commissioners to Commissioners of Irish Lights.

Harbour Commissioners Office, Cork,
2 July 1868.

Sir,

I am directed by the Cork Harbour Commissioners to acknowledge the receipt of your letter of the 20th ultimo, and copy of one from the Board of Trade, 23rd ultimo, in reference to the removal of Daunt's Rock.

I am, &c.

The Secretary,
Irish Lights Office, Dublin.

(signed)   *William Douryan,*
Secretary.

— No. 100. —

Commissioners of Irish Lights to Trinity House.

Irish Lights Office, Dublin,
16 April 1872.

Sir,

With reference to your letter of the 10th instant, on subject of Mr. Roche's proposed fog signal at Roche's Point, I am to acquaint you the Commissioners of Irish Lights have directed me to state they will feel much obliged if the Elder Brethren would be so good as to have inquiries made through their engineer, Mr. Douglass, as to the desirability of carrying out Mr. Roche's suggestion, inasmuch as the Commissioners have not sufficient information to enable them to come to a decision themselves.

I am, &c.

The Secretary, Trinity House.

(signed)   *W. Lees.*

See Back to No. 97.

— No. 101. —

Trinity House to Commissioners of Irish Lights.

Sir,   Trinity House, London, 24 April 1872.

I am directed to acknowledge the receipt of your letter of the 16th instant, requesting that inquiries may be made through Mr. Douglass as to the desirability of carrying out Mr. Roche's suggestion with reference to the proposed fog signal on Roche's Point, and, in reply, I am to acquaint you that the principle which has guided the Elder Brethren in the adoption of instruments connected with the lighthouse service, has been to require full particulars of the invention at the time under discussion, and that unless Mr. Roche is willing to submit the details of the proposed signal, the Elder Brethren do not see how Mr. Douglass can be in a position to advise thereon, although they will have great pleasure in consulting him, for the information of the Commissioners, if adequate data be given.

I am, &c.

The Secretary, Irish Lights Office.

(signed)   *Robin Allen.*

— No. 102. —

Commissioners of Irish Lights to Cork Harbour Commissioners.

Irish Lights Office, Dublin,
23 October 1872.

Sir,

With reference to the correspondence which has taken place as to the better marking of the approaches to Cork Harbour, I am directed by the Commissioners of Irish Lights to transmit copy of a letter from the Board of Trade, under date the 11th instant, enclosing letter from the Elder Brethren of the Trinity House

(copy)

Nos. 98 and 41.

(copy), and I have to request you will be so good as to move the Cork Harbour Commissioners to favour this Board with any observations they may have to offer thereon.

The Secretary, Harbour Board, Cork.

I am, &c.
(signed) W. Lees.

— No. 103. —

Cork Harbour Commissioners to Commissioners of Irish Lights.

Harbour Commissioners Office, Cork,
2 November 1872.

Sir,

With reference to your letters of the 23rd ultimo and 1st instant, relative to the better marking the approaches to Cork Harbour by means of fog signals, I am to acquaint you, for the information of the Commissioners of Irish Lights, that the correspondence enclosed therein has been referred to a Committee of this Board for consideration. Their Report shall be brought up at the earliest possible date, when you shall be fully informed of the views of the Board on the subject.

W. Lees, Esq.

I am, &c.
(signed) W. Dungan.

— No. 104. —

Trinity House to Commissioners of Irish Lights.

Extract from Letter from Trinity House to Commissioners of Irish Lights, under date the 8th February 1873 :

" Having laid before the Board your letter of the 24th ultimo, expressing the concurrence of the Commissioners of Irish Lights in the modification suggested by my letter of the 16th ultimo in the arrangement for marking the approaches to Cork Harbour, and also offering observations on the proposed changes in the marking of Lough Swilly, I am directed, with respect to the questions raised upon details of the first mentioned subject, to observe, that the intention of the Elder Brethren was, that the character of Roche's Point Light be retained exactly as at present, without extending the limits of the lower light, which would still remain as a mark to indicate the position of Daunt's Rock in case the proposed light vessel should drift. Also, as respects the holding ground in the vicinity of Daunt's Rock, the Board concur in the opinion that the nature of the ground in that locality should be ascertained, so as to remove any doubt the Commissioners may have upon the subject. The observations of Captain Sheppard have but little bearing on the question ; he does not give any certain data as to the ground outside the danger, and the Elder Brethren had no thought of recommending that the light vessel should be placed on the shore side of the Rock ; while his remarks as to her riding, would equally apply to any of the numerous light vessels now afloat in exposed situations. No doubt the ' Alexandra' steam vessel could, with a day or two's careful sounding and dredging, determine the general nature of the bottom, and find a suitable berth for mooring the ship."

— No. 105. —

Commissioners of Irish Lights to Trinity House.

Extract from Commissioners letter to Trinity House in reply to foregoing, under date 10th February 1873 :

" I have to state, the Board will instruct the Inspector of Lights to proceed as early as weather permits, and survey the ground outside Daunt's Rock, with reference to selecting the best position for mooring a light vessel."

Commissioners of Irish Lights to Trinity House.

Irish Lights Office, Dublin,
7 July 1873.

Sir,

With reference to previous correspondence on subject of marking the approaches to Cork Harbour, and more particularly to your letter of the 6th February last, and with regard to the suggestion of the Commissioners of Irish Lights, approved of by the Trinity House, that the nature of the holding ground in the vicinity of Daunt's Rock should be ascertained in connection with the proposition to place a light ship to mark that danger, I have to acquaint you, the Board directed their Inspector of Lights to take the earliest opportunity to survey the locality, and I have now to forward, for the information of the Elder Brethren, a report from Commander Hawes, r.n., together with a tracing showing the result of the soundings taken, the position of bell boat and buoy, also proposed position by him of light ship.

I am, &c.

The Secretary, Trinity House.
(signed)   W. Lees.

Enclosure in No. 106.

Irish Lights Office, Dublin,
13 June 1873.

Sir,

I beg herewith to forward a chart showing the soundings taken by me in the vicinity of and over Daunt's Rock; also the position I would propose for the light ship. Should the Board approve of this vessel being placed as suggested, the bell buoy could be removed, but I would recommend that the small buoy be left in its position, both as a mark for the rock and a marking buoy for the ship. The ship could be safely moored on this station the same as to other light vessels, by a single mushroom, if placed where proposed, free which, in case of parting her chain or breaking adrift, there would be very little chance of her going near the rock, which, except at dead low water and a heavy sea, she would not touch, even in going immediately over the rock. The ground between the Daunt's and Smith Rocks is nearly even, which shows it is not rock, but a plateau of sand brokn and large stones; in many places where the arming of the lead showed rock, on using the dredge I found to be large stones. The point at issue, viz., whether a light ship can be moored to mark this danger or not, may now be set at rest, as I am of opinion a ship would hold on there as well as they do at other places, and will be a much easier riding station than either the Cosling Bank or Conningbeg. Should the Board wish, one of our spare light vessels could be fitted and placed on that station before the winter sets in. I find that Daunt's Rock is about 160 yards long, and about 80 yards wide, and the shoalest spot on it to be 11 feet at low water ordinary spring tides.

I am, &c.

W. Lees, Esq., &c. &c.
(signed)   E. W. Hawes,
Inspector of Lights.

Cork Harbour Commissioners to Commissioners of Irish Lights.

Cork Harbour Commissioners Office,
Cork, 2 July 1873.

Sir,

With reference to previous correspondence on the subject of an efficient system of fog signalling at Roche's Point, Cork Harbour, I am directed by this Board to request that you will be so good as to acquaint me for their information, what progress has been made in the matter, the time when the signal will probably be erected, and the mode of signalling proposed to be adopted. The Commissioners consider this matter of urgent importance, and if delayed, may not fail to be attended with danger to the shipping frequenting the Port of Cork.

I am, &c.

W. Lees, Esq., &c., &c.
(signed)   Wm. Dorgan.

— No. 108. —

Commissioners of Irish Lights to Cork Harbour Commissioners.

Irish Lights Office, Dublin,
Sir, 13 July 1878.

Having submitted to the Commissioners of Irish Lights your letter of the 2nd instant, on subject of an efficient system of fog signals at Roche's Point, Cork Harbour, I am to inform you, the cause of the delay in erecting such fog signals to mark the approaches to Queenstown, is, that the Commissioners are waiting the result of a series of experiments which the Elder Brethren of the Trinity House have been for some time past engaged in carrying out, in order to ascertain the most efficient fog signal for the benefit of general shipping.

I am, &c.
Wm. Donegan. Esq., &c., &c., (signed) W. Lees
Cork.

— No. 109. —

Cork Harbour Commissioners to Commissioners of Irish Lights.

Harbour Commissioners, Cork,
Sir, 19 July 1878.

I am directed by this Board to request that you will bring under the notice of the Commissioners of Irish Lights, the advisability of altering the light at the entrance to Cork Harbour, so as to cause it to remain visible for 60 seconds, and obscured for 10 seconds, vice area being now the case. In making this suggestion to the Commissioners of Irish Lights, I am to state, that the Harbour Commissioners have been moved to do so, in consequence of a communication received from the Cork Steam Packet Company, who have been considering the subject, and that company has obtained the recommendation herein made from the masters in command of their various steamers, who are continually trading to and from the port. It is also the opinion of this Board, that for the present, pending the result of the inquiries of the Elder Brethren of the Trinity House, on the subject of providing efficient fog signals along the coast, that were a steam roarer, similar to that in use at Dungeness, placed on Poor Head, and a piece of ordnance placed at Roche's Point, the difficulty at present experienced by master mariners approaching Cork Harbour, and the dangers to which vessels are subjected in time of fog, would be considerably removed.

I am, &c.
W. Lees, Esq., &c., &c. (signed) Wm. Donegan.

— No. 110. —

Commissioners of Irish Lights to Cork Harbour Commissioners.

Irish Lights Office, Dublin,
Sir, 6 August 1878.

In reference to your letter of the 19th ultimo, on subject of the better marking of the approaches to Cork Harbour, I am to acquaint you that arrangements are now being made by the Commissioners of Irish Lights with the Board of Trade and Trinity House with a view to carrying out the improvements in the lights and signals in the vicinity of Cork Harbour.

I am, &c.
Wm. Donegan, Esq. (signed) W. Lees.

— No. 111. —

Commissioners of Irish Lights to Cork Harbour Commissioners.

Irish Lights Office, Dublin,
2 October 1872.

Sir,

WITH reference to my letters of the 12th July and 8th August, relative to the proposed better marking of the approaches to Cork Harbour, I am directed to acquaint you, for the information of the Cork Harbour Board, that the Elder Brethren of the Trinity House have intimated to this Board that as yet they have been unable to arrive at any definite conclusion as to the most efficient description of fog signal, and therefore purpose carrying out further experiments at the South Foreland.

I am, &c.

Wm. Donegan, Esq., Cork.   (signed)   W. Lea.

— No. 112. —

Cork Harbour Commissioners to Commissioners of Irish Lights.

Harbour Commissioners Office, Cork,
10 October 1872.

Sir,

I AM to acknowledge the receipt of your letter, dated 2nd instant, stating that as yet the Elder Brethren of the Trinity House have been unable to arrive at any definite conclusion as to the most efficient description of fog signals to be adopted for marking the approaches to Cork Harbour. I am directed by this Board to invite reference to my letter dated 19th July last, and to request that the Commissioners of Irish Lights may be induced to carry out promptly the recommendation therein contained. The Harbour Commissioners desire to state, that the continued postponement by the Elder Brethren in determining the system of fog signals along the coast in proximity to Cork Harbour, cannot fail to be detrimental to the interest of vessels frequenting the port; and with this view the Commissioners trust the Commissioners of Irish Lights will see good reasons for adopting, at least for the present, the recommendation already suggested by them in their letter herein referred to.

I am, &c.

Wm. Lea, Esq., &c., &c.   (signed)   Wm. Donegan.

— No. 113. —

Commissioners of Irish Lights to Cork Harbour Commissioners.

Irish Lights Office, Dublin,
11 October 1872.

Sir,

I HAVE leave to acknowledge your letter of the 10th instant, on the subject of steps being taken to alter the character of the Roche's Point Light, as referred to in your letter of the 19th July, and in reply I beg to inform you this matter will be carefully considered when the final arrangements are being made for the better marking the approaches to Cork Harbour.

I am, &c.

W. Donegan, Esq., &c., &c.,   (signed)   W. Lea.
    Cork.

— No. 114. —

Commissioners of Irish Lights to Cork Harbour Commissioners.

Irish Lights Office, Dublin,
Sir, 20 October 1873.

I am directed by the Commissioners of Irish Lights to acknowledge the receipt of your letter of the 10th instant, and in reply to state they are quite alive to the necessity of improving the approaches to Cork Harbour. In order to do so they have applied, through the Trinity House, to the Board of Trade, to sanction a light ship being placed to mark Daunt's Rock, having on board a fog trumpet: the light at Roche's Point to be increased in power, with a large fog bell at the station: a powerful fog horn to be put on Poer Head.

The Trinity Brethren not having yet completed their experiments with fog signals, the Commissioners recognising the advisability of no further delay occurring, have requested permission of the Board of Trade to allow them to at once place the best description of fog signal at present known. I am to add, it is in contemplation to improve the light on the Old Head of Kinsale; and I am further to observe, that the suggestion contained in your letter of the 19th July last, as to an alteration in the revolution of the Roche's Point Light, will be carefully considered.

I am, &c.
W. Donegan, Esq., &c., &c., (signed) W. Lees.
Cork.

— No. 115. —

Cork Harbour Commissioners to Commissioners of Irish Lights.

Harbour Commissioners Office, Cork,
Sir, 25 October 1873.

I am directed by the Cork Harbour Commissioners to acknowledge the receipt of your letter of the 20th instant, pointing out the improvements intended to be made by the Commissioners of Lights, and for which the sanction of the Board of Trade has been invited, for the better marking the approaches to Cork Harbour, and to state in reply, that the Commissioners consider the decision arrived at by the Commissioners of Irish Lights cannot fail to prove of advantage to passing vessels.

I am, &c.
W. Lees, Esq., &c., &c. (signed) W. Donegan.

— No. 116. —

Trinity House to Commissioners of Irish Lights.

London, 21 November 1873.
Sir,

Referring to previous correspondence on the subject of the better marking of the approaches to Cork Harbour, I am now directed to hand you, for the information of the Commissioners of Irish Lights, the accompanying copy of a letter and its enclosure which has been received from the Board of Trade thereon, and in which is conveyed the statutory sanction of that Department to the scheme which had already been agreed upon by your Commissioners and this Corporation, as follows :—

1st. A light vessel to be placed off Daunt's Rock, showing a powerful fixed red light and to be fitted with a powerful fog trumpet.

2nd. Roche's Point to be, as at present, red revolving, but to be changed from

from catoptric to dioptric of the 2nd order; a lower light (fixed white) remaining as at present to mark Daunt's Rock.

3rd. A powerful fog trumpet to be placed on Poer Head.

4th. The Light at the Old Head of Kinsale to be increased in power.

I am, &c.

W. Lees, Esq.,   (signed)   Robin Allen.
Irish Lights Office, Dublin.

Enclosure in No. 116.

(Similar to No. 72.)

— No. 117. —

Commissioners of Irish Lights to Trinity House.

Irish Lights Office, Dublin,
1 December 1873.

Sir,

WITH reference to your letter, forwarding drawings and specifications for a wooden light vessel of an improved description, constructed in 1851, I am to state, my Board will feel further obliged if the Elder Brethren will favour them with any additional drawings, &c. for the most improved description of light ship since 1851, and on board which the most improved fog horn has been fitted, with the name of patentee. The above information is solicited, having for its object the placing of a light ship, with powerful fog horn or trumpet, to mark Daunt's Rock. An early reply will much oblige.

I am, &c.

R. Allen, Esq.,   (signed)   W. Lees.
Trinity House, London.

— No. 118. —

Trinity House to Commissioners of Irish Lights.

EXTRACT from Letter from Trinity House, under date the 15th December 1873, in Reply to Commissioners' Letter to Elder Brethren, dated 1st same Month.

" WITH regard to the trumpet and fog horn apparatus which are now in use on board a few of the light vessels, I have to acquaint you that at the present time the Elder Brethren, with the assistance of Professor Tyndall, have their attention directed to experiments, the result of which will probably lead to the adoption of a more powerful fog signal than either of those now in use. Until the experiments in question have been concluded, the Elder Brethren are not desirous of recommending for adoption by your Board the signals before referred to."

www.ingramcontent.com/pod-product-compliance
Lightning Source LLC
Chambersburg PA
CBHW031456270326
41930CB00007B/1026